Joker: Folie à Deux

The Ultimate Guide to the 2024 Cinematic Masterpiece

By

Jackson Sanderson

© July 2024 by Jackson Sanderson

All rights reserved. This book is solely the creation of Jackson Sanderson, and no part of it may be reproduced, distributed, or transmitted in any form or by any means, be it photocopying, recording, or other electronic or mechanical methods, without the prior written permission of the publisher. However, short quotations for critical reviews and certain noncommercial uses allowed by copyright law are exceptions.

For inquiries about permissions, please reach out to:

Jackson Sanderson Contact Email: JacksonSanderson@gmail.com

TABLE OF CONTENT

Introduction
  Overview of the Joker Legacy
  The Hype Around "Folie à Deux"
Chapter 1: The Making of "Joker: Folie à Deux"
  Development and Announcement
  Key Production Details
  Filming Locations and Techniques
Chapter 2: The Cast and Characters
  Joaquin Phoenix as Arthur Fleck/Joker
  Lady Gaga's Role and Influence
  Supporting Cast and Their Characters
Chapter 3: Themes and Inspirations
  Psychological Elements
  Musical Influence and Themes
  Connection to the First Joker Movie
Chapter 4: Behind the Scenes
  Director Todd Phillips' Vision
  Screenwriting and Story Development
  Cinematography and Visual Style
Chapter 5: Music and Soundtrack
  Composers and Key Tracks
  The Role of Music in the Narrative
  Analysis of Key Musical Moments
Chapter 6: Marketing and Promotion
  Trailers and Teasers
  Social Media Campaigns
  Press Coverage and Interviews
Chapter 7: Fan Theories and Predictions

   Popular Fan Theories
   Speculations on the Plot
   Audience Expectations

Chapter 8: Critical Reception and Box Office
   Early Reviews and Critiques
   Box Office Performance
   Comparisons to Other Joker Films

Chapter 9: Impact and Legacy
   Influence on Pop Culture
   Future of the Joker Franchise
   Reflections on the Movie's Place in Cinema History

Conclusion
   Final Thoughts
   What to Expect Next

Appendices
   Key Interviews and Quotes
   Additional Resources and Reading

Introduction
Overview of the Joker Legacy

In the sprawling annals of comic book lore, few characters have carved a niche as indelible and as perversely captivating as the Joker. His legacy, a chaotic symphony of laughter and lunacy, spans over eight decades, touching the hearts, minds, and nightmares of audiences across the globe. The Clown Prince of Crime, with his grotesque grin and maniacal mirth, has evolved from a mere comic book villain to a cultural icon, a mirror reflecting the darkest recesses of the human psyche.

Our tale begins in the early 1940s, a golden age for superheroes, when Batman was still a fledgling figure in the caped crusader community. Created by Bill Finger, Bob Kane, and Jerry Robinson, the Joker first appeared in Batman #1 in 1940. Initially conceived as a sinister court jester, the Joker's early incarnation was one of unrestrained malevolence, a stark contrast to the relatively sanitized villains of the time. His debut was marked by a series of gruesome murders, each punctuated by his mocking laughter—a harbinger of the complex character he would become.

The 1950s brought about the Comics Code Authority, a regulatory body that sought to sanitize comic book content. Under its influence, the Joker was transformed from a murderous psychopath into a buffoonish prankster, his sharp edges dulled by censorship. This era, while less thrilling in terms of narrative complexity, laid the groundwork for the character's adaptability—a trait that would prove crucial in his enduring legacy.

Fast forward to the 1960s, and the Joker's fortune took another turn with the advent of the Batman television series. Cesar Romero's portrayal of the Joker was a kaleidoscope of colors and camp, his painted-over mustache a quirky testament to the era's whimsical approach to the character. This version of the Joker was flamboyant, theatrical, and above all, fun—a far cry from his darker origins but equally memorable. Romero's performance etched the Joker into the collective consciousness of a new generation, proving that the character could thrive in a variety of interpretations.

The pendulum swung back to darkness in the 1970s and 1980s, as comic book storytelling matured and grew more sophisticated. Dennis O'Neil and Neal Adams redefined the Joker in their seminal work, restoring his homicidal tendencies and psychological depth. This period gave birth to some of the most iconic Joker stories, including "The Joker's Five-Way Revenge," which reestablished him as Batman's arch-nemesis. The climax of this dark renaissance came with Alan Moore and Brian Bolland's "The Killing Joke" in 1988, a graphic novel that delved deep into the Joker's psyche and presented his origin story as a tragic tale of one bad day gone horribly wrong. This work not only cemented the Joker's place as a complex, multifaceted villain but also influenced subsequent portrayals in significant ways.

As the pages of comic books continued to turn, the Joker's presence expanded beyond the confines of print. Tim Burton's 1989 film "Batman" introduced the Joker to the silver screen with Jack Nicholson donning the clown's chaotic countenance. Nicholson's portrayal was a masterclass in madness, blending the character's theatricality with a menacing edge that captivated audiences. His Joker was both charming and chilling, a perfect embodiment of the character's dual nature.

The 1990s saw the Joker's dominance continue in "Batman: The Animated Series," where Mark Hamill's voice performance brought a new dimension to the character. Hamill's Joker was a tour de force of vocal dynamism, ranging from gleeful cackles to sinister growls. This iteration combined the dark, psychological aspects of the character with a more nuanced, almost tragic depth, resonating with both children and adults alike. The series itself became a benchmark for animated storytelling, and

Hamill's Joker remains a definitive portrayal to this day.

The new millennium ushered in a more visceral, grounded take on the Joker with Christopher Nolan's "The Dark Knight" in 2008. Heath Ledger's performance, posthumously awarded an Academy Award, was nothing short of transformative. His Joker was anarchic, nihilistic, and utterly terrifying, a portrayal that redefined the character for a modern audience. Ledger's methodical immersion into the role created a Joker who was as intellectually formidable as he was violently unpredictable, a force of nature who challenged Batman not just physically but ideologically. This performance set a new standard for the character and left an indelible mark on popular culture.

The Joker's journey through the early 21st century continued with varied portrayals, each bringing something new to the table. Jared Leto's Joker in "Suicide Squad" (2016) offered a controversial, heavily stylized version of the character, complete with tattoos and a more modern gangster aesthetic. Though divisive, Leto's interpretation highlighted the character's malleability and the myriad ways in which he could be reimagined.

Then came Joaquin Phoenix's turn in Todd Phillips' "Joker" (2019), a film that took a bold, introspective approach to the character. Phoenix's Joker was not a villain in the traditional sense but rather a tragic figure, a victim of societal neglect and personal trauma. The film's raw, unflinching portrayal of Arthur Fleck's descent into madness resonated deeply with audiences and critics alike, earning Phoenix an Academy Award for Best Actor. This portrayal underscored the Joker's potential as a vehicle for exploring complex social and psychological themes, proving that the character could be both timeless and timely.

As we arrive at 2024, the legacy of the Joker continues to evolve with "Joker: Folie à Deux." Anticipation is high, not only because of the success of the previous film but also due to the intriguing addition of Lady Gaga, whose role promises to bring yet another layer of complexity to the narrative. This new chapter in the Joker's saga is poised to delve deeper into the character's psyche, exploring the chaotic dance between sanity and madness, reality and delusion.

The Joker's enduring appeal lies in his ability to adapt, to mirror the fears and anxieties of each generation while maintaining his core essence of anarchic unpredictability. From the pages of comic books to the bright lights of Hollywood, the Joker has remained a fascinating enigma, a character who defies easy categorization and continues to captivate and disturb in equal measure. As we look back on his storied past and forward to his future, one thing is certain: the Joker's legacy is far from over, and his maniacal laughter will echo through the corridors of time, forever reminding us of the thin line between order and chaos, sanity and madness.

The Hype Around "Folie à Deux"

The air crackles with anticipation as "Joker: Folie à Deux" looms on the cinematic horizon, promising a return to the dark, chaotic world that left audiences both mesmerized and disturbed in 2019. Since its announcement, the sequel has been a hotbed of speculation, excitement, and feverish expectation. Fans, critics, and industry insiders alike are on tenterhooks, eagerly dissecting every morsel of information that trickles out. This collective buzz is not merely about a film; it's a testament to the Joker's unyielding grip on our imaginations.

The first rumblings of "Joker: Folie à Deux" began as whispers in the wind, tantalizing hints that Joaquin Phoenix would once again don the harlequin's mask. The original "Joker" was a cultural phenomenon, a tour de force that grossed over a billion dollars and earned Phoenix an Oscar for his haunting portrayal of Arthur Fleck. The prospect of a sequel was, from the outset, both thrilling and fraught with high expectations. Would it live up to its predecessor? Could it delve even deeper into the psyche of its tormented protagonist? These questions fueled a fervor that only grew with time.

When the official announcement was made, the internet erupted in a cacophony of joy and speculation. Social media platforms became a playground for theories and predictions. Reddit threads stretched into the thousands as fans debated potential plotlines, character arcs, and thematic elements. Twitter buzzed with excitement, with hashtags like #Joker2 and #FolieADeux trending worldwide. Instagram became a gallery of fan art, memes, and speculative posts, each more imaginative than the last.

The release of the first teaser trailer was a masterstroke of marketing, a tantalizing glimpse into the chaos to come. The trailer opens with a haunting melody, a solitary piano note echoing through a dimly lit room. Joaquin Phoenix's Arthur Fleck, now fully transformed into the Joker, stares into a cracked mirror, his reflection a mosaic of fractured sanity. Enter Lady Gaga, her character shrouded in mystery but exuding a magnetic, almost dangerous allure. The brief yet powerful scenes showcased in the trailer hinted at a narrative steeped in psychological complexity and dark humor. Fans dissected every frame, hunting for clues and hidden meanings, their excitement palpable and infectious.

Lady Gaga's involvement added another layer of intrigue and anticipation. Known for her theatricality and intense performances, Gaga's casting sparked a flurry of discussions. Would she be a new villain, a twisted love interest, or something entirely unexpected? Her enigmatic presence in the trailer, coupled with her past success in "A Star is Born," where she showcased her acting chops alongside her musical talent, suggested that her role in "Folie à Deux" would be nothing short of spectacular. Her cryptic social media posts only added fuel to the fire, each one dissected for potential hints about her character and the film's plot.

Industry expectations for "Joker: Folie à Deux" are sky-high. The original "Joker" not only shattered box office records but also set a new benchmark for what a comic book film could achieve, blending gritty realism with profound psychological insights. Todd Phillips, the visionary director behind the first film, returns with a bold vision for the sequel. Early reports suggest that "Folie à Deux" will delve deeper into the themes of madness and identity, exploring the symbiotic relationship between Joker and his surroundings, and perhaps even introducing elements of musical storytelling, a daring departure from traditional narrative forms.

Critics and analysts are eager to see how Phillips and Phoenix navigate the treacherous waters of sequel-making. There's an understanding that "Folie à Deux" must balance the familiar with the innovative, building on the foundation of its predecessor while forging new paths. The film's title, "Folie à Deux," a term referring to shared psychosis, hints at a complex, intertwined narrative that promises to challenge and engage audiences on multiple levels.

The promotional campaign for "Folie à Deux" has been nothing short of genius. From cryptic posters that tease the film's dark themes to meticulously crafted social media campaigns, every element has been designed to stoke the fires of anticipation. Behind-the-scenes photos and interviews with the cast and crew have provided just enough insight to keep fans on the edge of their seats without giving away too much. This careful balance of mystery and revelation has created a potent cocktail of excitement and speculation.

Moreover, the film has generated significant buzz within the industry. Insiders have praised Phillips' bold direction and Phoenix's immersive performance. There's talk of "Folie à Deux" being a serious contender in the upcoming awards season, with early screenings reportedly leaving audiences in awe. The involvement of Lady Gaga, both as an actress and a possible contributor to the film's soundtrack, has only heightened expectations, promising a multi-sensory experience that transcends conventional genre boundaries.

As the release date approaches, the hype shows no signs of abating. Fans are organizing viewing parties, creating elaborate cosplay costumes, and even holding themed events to celebrate the film's arrival. The shared anticipation has fostered a sense of community among Joker enthusiasts, a testament to the character's enduring appeal and the film's potential impact.

"Joker: Folie à Deux" stands poised to not only meet but exceed the lofty expectations set by its predecessor. The excitement surrounding the film is a testament to the powerful storytelling and complex characters that Phillips, Phoenix, and now Gaga are bringing to life. As we inch closer to its release, one thing is clear: "Folie à Deux" is not just a film—it's a cultural event, a shared experience that promises to captivate, challenge, and enthrall. The Joker's laughter echoes once more, and the world waits with bated breath to see what new madness will unfold.

Chapter 1: The Making of "Joker: Folie à Deux"
Development and Announcement

In the shadowy corridors of Hollywood, where whispers echo louder than shouts and secrets are currency, the tale of "Joker: Folie à Deux" began not with a bang but a murmur. The year was 2019, and the original "Joker" had just stormed the cinematic landscape, leaving in its wake a trail of astonished audiences and bewildered critics. Joaquin Phoenix's chilling portrayal of Arthur Fleck—a man unraveling into madness amidst the decay of Gotham—had not only won him an Oscar but also rekindled the dark allure of the Joker. As the film raked in accolades and box office gold, the question on everyone's lips was inevitable: would there be a sequel?

The initial rumors were like smoke, elusive and intangible, swirling in the aether of industry gossip. Todd Phillips, the maverick director behind "Joker," had always been coy about the prospect of a follow-up. In interviews, he danced around the topic with the finesse of a seasoned performer, acknowledging the demand while cautioning against the perils of a rushed sequel. "Joker," after all, had been conceived as a standalone masterpiece, a grim character study rather than the first chapter of a sprawling franchise. Yet, as days turned to weeks and weeks to months, the whispers grew louder, fueled by cryptic hints and speculative articles.

The first substantial clue came in the form of a leaked document—a tantalizing tidbit that sent the internet into a frenzy. It was a simple memo, purportedly from Warner Bros., referencing an upcoming project code-named "Folie." Fans and pundits alike pounced on this morsel, dissecting it with forensic zeal. Was this the long-awaited sequel? What did "Folie" signify? The term, French for "madness," seemed a fitting nod to the Joker's chaotic essence, but it was the second part, "à Deux," that intrigued the most. Shared madness. A duet of insanity. The possibilities were as intoxicating as they were numerous.

The official confirmation came not through a grandiose press conference but via a social media post—modern Hollywood's answer to a royal decree. Todd Phillips, ever the showman, chose Instagram as his stage. The post was a study in minimalism: a photograph of the script's cover page, with the title "Joker: Folie à Deux" emblazoned in stark, black letters. Beside it, a cryptic caption—"It begins." The response was immediate and explosive. Within minutes, the post garnered thousands of likes and comments, a digital roar of approval and anticipation. News outlets scrambled to break the story, and social media platforms buzzed with renewed fervor.

With the cat officially out of the bag, the early production stages of "Folie à Deux" began in earnest. Todd Phillips, alongside screenwriter Scott Silver, retreated into the creative cocoon, crafting a story that would not only honor the original but also push the boundaries of the Joker mythos. Their task was Herculean: to expand the narrative while preserving the intimate, character-driven essence that had defined the first film. In interviews, Phillips spoke of the challenge with a mix of excitement and trepidation. "We didn't want to just make a sequel," he explained. "We wanted to explore new territory, to delve deeper into Arthur's psyche and the world around him."

One of the most significant and buzzworthy developments was the casting of Lady Gaga. The announcement came shrouded in the same tantalizing mystery that had characterized the project thus far. An enigmatic tweet from Gaga, a single word—"Folie"—accompanied by a Joker card emoji. The internet exploded once more. Speculation ran rampant. Would she be playing Harley Quinn, the Joker's notorious accomplice and lover? Or perhaps an entirely new character, one who would bring a fresh dynamic to the twisted tale? The potential of Gaga's theatrical prowess, combined with her proven acting chops, set imaginations ablaze.

As casting news trickled out, the ensemble began to take shape. Familiar faces from the first film were confirmed to return, alongside new additions that promised to bring even more depth and complexity to the narrative. Each casting announcement was met with a wave of enthusiasm, the anticipation building like a symphony reaching its crescendo. Production photos began to surface, offering glimpses of the actors in character, the sets, the mood. These images, often leaked by intrepid paparazzi or shared by the cast and crew themselves, were pored over by fans eager for any hint of what was to come.

The production design, a crucial element of "Joker's" success, was once again helmed by Mark Friedberg. His vision of Gotham —a city teetering on the edge of collapse, rife with decay and despair—had been a character in its own right. For "Folie à Deux," Friedberg sought to build upon this foundation, creating an environment that mirrored Arthur Fleck's fractured mind. Early reports spoke of elaborate set pieces, meticulously crafted to evoke both wonder and unease. The attention to detail, from the graffiti-strewn alleyways to the dimly lit interiors, was nothing short of obsessive, each element contributing to the film's immersive atmosphere.

Filming officially began in late 2022, under a shroud of secrecy befitting the Joker's enigmatic nature. The set was a fortress, with security measures in place to prevent leaks and spoilers. Despite these efforts, snippets of information inevitably found their way into the public domain. Joaquin Phoenix was spotted on location, his transformation into Arthur Fleck as startling and haunting as ever. Lady Gaga, too, was seen in character, her presence electric, her costume and makeup hinting at a role as complex and captivating as Phoenix's Joker.

The first teaser trailer, released in mid-2023, was a masterclass in suspense and intrigue. Clocking in at just under two minutes, it offered a tantalizing glimpse into the madness of "Folie à Deux." The footage was a montage of haunting images and cryptic scenes, set to a dissonant, almost hypnotic score. Arthur Fleck, now fully embraced by his Joker persona, moved through a world that seemed both familiar and alien. Lady Gaga's character was introduced with a fleeting shot—her eyes alight with a mix of passion and madness, her smile a mirror to Arthur's own. The trailer ended with a chilling laugh, echoing into darkness, leaving viewers both captivated and craving more.

Throughout this period, the film's marketing campaign expertly balanced revelation and mystery. The promotional materials —posters, interviews, and social media posts—were carefully curated to maintain the film's enigmatic allure. Todd Phillips and the cast engaged with fans through select media appearances, offering just enough insight to whet appetites without giving away the game. This strategy paid off in spades, as anticipation for "Folie à Deux" continued to build to a fever pitch.

As 2024 dawned, the buzz around "Joker: Folie à Deux" reached a crescendo. Industry insiders and fans alike speculated on the film's potential impact. Would it match the critical and commercial success of its predecessor? Could Phoenix and Gaga's performances capture the same lightning in a bottle that had made the original "Joker" such a phenomenon? Early screenings and test reactions hinted at a resounding yes, with reports of standing ovations and rave reviews.

In the months leading up to the release, the cast and crew embarked on a global promotional tour, sharing insights and experiences from the set. Joaquin Phoenix, known for his intense dedication to his roles, spoke of the challenges and rewards of returning to Arthur Fleck's tortured mind. Lady Gaga, ever the consummate performer, teased her character's arc with a mix of enthusiasm and mystery, her interviews peppered with hints that only fueled further speculation.

The making of "Joker: Folie à Deux" was a journey marked by creativity, collaboration, and a touch of madness. From the initial whispers to the final, frenzied push towards release, the film's development was a testament to the power of storytelling and the enduring allure of the Joker. As audiences around the world awaited the curtain to rise on this next chapter, one thing was clear: "Folie à Deux" was poised to leave an indelible mark on the cinematic landscape, echoing the chaotic brilliance of its predecessor while forging new, unforgettable paths.

Key Production Details

The Creative Team

At the helm of "Joker: Folie à Deux" stands the indomitable Todd Phillips, whose vision for the Joker saga has proven both revolutionary and revelatory. Phillips, alongside screenwriter Scott Silver, crafted a narrative that delved into the fractured psyche of Arthur Fleck, transforming a comic book villain into a tragic, almost Shakespearean figure. Their collaboration was instrumental in the first film's success, blending gritty realism with poignant storytelling, and it was clear from the outset that this creative duo would be essential for the sequel.

Phillips' direction is characterized by a meticulous attention to detail and an ability to elicit powerful performances from his actors. Known for his versatility, having directed everything from comedies like "The Hangover" to intense dramas like "War Dogs," Phillips brought a unique sensibility to "Joker," balancing the bleakness of Fleck's world with moments of dark humor and profound humanity. For "Folie à Deux," Phillips aimed to build on this foundation, exploring new thematic territories while preserving the raw emotional core that resonated so deeply with audiences.

Scott Silver, a seasoned screenwriter whose credits include "8 Mile" and "The Fighter," once again partnered with Phillips to pen the script. Silver's knack for crafting compelling, character-driven narratives was crucial in shaping the story of Arthur Fleck. Together, Phillips and Silver envisioned "Folie à Deux" as a deeper dive into the complexities of shared madness, exploring how the Joker's insanity might influence and be influenced by those around him.

The Budget

The financial landscape of "Joker: Folie à Deux" reflects the high stakes and grand ambitions of the project. The original "Joker," with its relatively modest budget of $55 million, had been a financial juggernaut, grossing over a billion dollars worldwide. This success granted the sequel a significantly larger budget, estimated at around $120 million. This increase allowed for greater creative freedom, enabling the filmmakers to expand their vision without the constraints that often accompany lower-budget productions.

The augmented budget facilitated several key aspects of the production. It enabled more elaborate set designs, advanced special effects, and a broader range of locations. Additionally, it allowed the filmmakers to attract top-tier talent, both in front of and behind the camera. The financial backing also provided the means to implement stringent security measures, ensuring that the details of the plot and key scenes remained shrouded in mystery until the film's release.

Logistical Challenges

Despite the robust budget and experienced creative team, the production of "Joker: Folie à Deux" faced numerous logistical challenges. Filming a high-profile sequel, particularly one with the cultural significance of "Joker," required navigating a labyrinth of potential pitfalls, from security concerns to scheduling conflicts and the ever-present specter of public scrutiny.

Security and Secrecy

Maintaining secrecy was paramount. The production team went to extraordinary lengths to prevent leaks, employing a range of tactics to keep details under wraps. Scripts were closely guarded, with only key personnel granted access. Digital copies were encrypted, and physical copies were watermarked and numbered. On set, security was tight, with personnel required to sign non-disclosure agreements and adhere to strict confidentiality protocols. These measures were designed to preserve the film's surprises and prevent spoilers from diluting the audience's experience.

Scheduling and Coordination

Scheduling posed another significant challenge. Coordinating the availability of high-profile actors like Joaquin Phoenix and Lady Gaga required meticulous planning. Phoenix, known for his immersive approach to acting, committed fully to the role, necessitating a schedule that accommodated his intense preparation and performance demands. Lady Gaga, juggling her music career alongside her burgeoning acting endeavors, also required a schedule that balanced her various commitments.

Filming took place across multiple locations, each chosen to enhance the film's atmospheric authenticity. Gotham City, a character in its own right, was brought to life through a combination of practical sets and real-world locations, primarily in New York City and Chicago. The logistical complexities of shooting in these bustling urban environments required careful coordination with local authorities, residents, and businesses to minimize disruption while capturing the desired aesthetic.

Creative and Technical Innovations

The expanded budget allowed for significant advancements in the film's technical aspects. Cinematographer Lawrence Sher, who had worked with Phillips on the original "Joker," returned to lend his visual expertise. Sher's cinematography on the first film was widely acclaimed for its evocative use of light and shadow, creating a visually striking representation of Arthur Fleck's descent into madness. For "Folie à Deux," Sher aimed to push the boundaries even further, experimenting with new techniques and technologies to capture the film's heightened emotional and psychological landscapes.

The use of cutting-edge special effects and practical effects also played a crucial role. The original film's practical effects had contributed to its gritty realism, and "Folie à Deux" sought to build on this foundation. Advanced CGI was employed to create seamless, visually arresting sequences, while practical effects ensured a tangible, immersive experience for both the actors and the audience.

Musical Elements

One of the most intriguing aspects of "Folie à Deux" was the integration of musical elements, a bold departure from the first film's more straightforward narrative style. The inclusion of Lady Gaga, renowned for her musical prowess, suggested that the sequel would explore new, innovative storytelling techniques. Reports indicated that the film would incorporate musical numbers, using them as a narrative device to delve deeper into the characters' psyches. This approach required a delicate balance, ensuring that the musical elements enhanced rather than overshadowed the core story.

The film's score, composed once again by Hildur Guðnadóttir, promised to be a highlight. Guðnadóttir's haunting, evocative music for the first "Joker" had been a critical component of its success, earning her an Academy Award. For "Folie à Deux," she sought to expand on the original themes while introducing new motifs to reflect the evolving narrative. Her collaboration with Lady Gaga, potentially contributing original songs to the soundtrack, added another layer of depth and complexity to the film's auditory landscape.

The Cast and Crew Dynamic

The dynamic between the cast and crew was a crucial factor in the film's production. Joaquin Phoenix's dedication to his craft set the tone, inspiring the entire team to push their creative boundaries. Phoenix, known for his method acting, immersed himself in the role of Arthur Fleck, maintaining character even off-camera to deliver an authentic performance. His commitment created an intense, focused atmosphere on set, fostering a sense of camaraderie and mutual respect among the cast and crew.

Lady Gaga's involvement brought a fresh energy and perspective. Her background in music and performance art influenced her approach to acting, blending theatricality with emotional depth. Gaga's willingness to take creative risks resonated with Phillips' vision, encouraging a collaborative spirit that permeated the production. The chemistry between Phoenix and Gaga, both on and off-screen, was palpable, adding a dynamic, electrifying quality to their performances.

The supporting cast, a mix of returning actors and new faces, contributed to the film's rich tapestry. Zazie Beetz reprised her role as Sophie Dumond, offering continuity and further development of her character's relationship with Arthur. New additions, carefully selected to complement the evolving narrative, brought fresh perspectives and added complexity to the story. Each actor's unique approach and interpretation of their roles enriched the film, creating a layered, multifaceted portrayal of Gotham's inhabitants.

Filming Locations and Techniques

The magic of "Joker: Folie à Deux" began in places that echoed with the essence of Gotham City's decay and vibrancy, capturing the duality of beauty and despair, grandeur and ruin. The locations chosen for the film were not mere backdrops but characters in their own right, each contributing to the narrative's texture and depth.

New York City: The Heart of Gotham

New York City, with its towering skyscrapers and labyrinthine streets, once again served as the primary stand-in for Gotham. There is a haunting poetry in the juxtaposition of New York's opulence and its shadows, a duality that mirrors Arthur Fleck's own fractured psyche. From the outset, Todd Phillips envisioned Gotham as a character—a living, breathing entity that interacts with its inhabitants, shaping and being shaped by their actions. New York provided the perfect canvas for this vision.

The film's production scoured the city for locations that would amplify the story's themes. Times Square, with its dazzling lights and relentless hustle, was a key location. Here, the Joker's anarchic energy collided with the city's pulsating life force. Filming in Times Square presented logistical challenges—navigating crowds, securing permits, and coordinating with local authorities—but the result was a series of scenes that buzzed with kinetic energy.

Another significant location was the Bronx, where the infamous stairway scene from the first film had become an iconic symbol of Arthur Fleck's transformation. Revisiting these stairs in "Folie à Deux" provided a sense of continuity while allowing for new creative explorations. The surrounding neighborhoods, with their mix of grit and resilience, offered a visually rich tapestry for the film's darker moments.

Chicago: The Grit of Gotham

Complementing New York's grandeur, Chicago brought its own

brand of urban grit to the portrayal of Gotham. Known for its architectural marvels and storied history, Chicago's streets and alleys provided a perfect blend of menace and mystique. The city's iconic L train, snaking above and below ground, became a metaphorical journey into the depths of Arthur's mind. Filming on the train and in the adjacent stations required precise choreography and timing, but the payoff was a series of visually striking sequences that heightened the film's tension and drama.

Chicago's Lower Wacker Drive, with its subterranean labyrinth of tunnels and roadways, was another key location. This underworld, bathed in eerie, flickering light, served as a tangible representation of Arthur's descent into madness. The production team utilized the natural chiaroscuro of the setting, employing minimal artificial lighting to enhance the shadows and create a claustrophobic, oppressive atmosphere.

Soundstages: Crafting the Intimate and the Grand

While real-world locations provided the raw material, much of "Joker: Folie à Deux" came to life on meticulously crafted soundstages. These controlled environments allowed for an unparalleled level of detail and precision. The production design team, led by Mark Friedberg, recreated iconic locations from the first film while introducing new sets that reflected Arthur's evolving world.

One of the most ambitious sets was Arkham Asylum, reimagined to reflect the twisted labyrinth of Arthur's mind. The asylum's stark, institutional corridors contrasted with the chaotic, colorful interior of Arthur's cell, a visual metaphor for the conflict between order and madness. The design team employed a mix of traditional set-building techniques and modern digital effects, creating a seamless blend that was both immersive and unsettling.

Innovative Filming Techniques

The technical prowess behind "Folie à Deux" was as significant as the locations themselves. Director of Photography Lawrence Sher, returning from the first film, pushed the boundaries of visual storytelling, experimenting with new techniques to capture the film's unique aesthetic.

Dynamic Camera Work

One of the most notable innovations was the use of dynamic camera work to mirror Arthur's psychological state. Handheld cameras were employed during intense, chaotic scenes, providing a raw, immediate feel that drew audiences into Arthur's perspective. In contrast, static, symmetrical shots were used in moments of eerie calm, creating a dissonance that heightened the film's tension.

Lighting and Color

Lighting played a crucial role in establishing the film's mood and tone. Natural light was favored whenever possible, lending an authenticity to the urban environments. However, strategic use of artificial lighting was employed to create dramatic contrasts and highlight key emotional beats. Neon lights, casting garish hues of red, green, and purple, bathed the night scenes, reflecting the Joker's flamboyant yet sinister persona.

Color grading was another essential tool, with the film's palette shifting from the muted, desaturated tones of Arthur's mundane life to the vibrant, almost hallucinogenic colors of his Joker persona. This visual evolution paralleled Arthur's psychological transformation, with each hue carefully chosen to evoke specific emotions and themes.

Practical and Special Effects

Practical effects were favored to maintain the film's gritty realism. Explosions, stunts, and physical transformations were executed in-camera whenever possible, enhancing the tangible, visceral quality of the action. For more complex sequences, state-of-the-art CGI was seamlessly integrated, ensuring that the effects served the story without overpowering it.

One of the most innovative uses of CGI involved the musical elements introduced in "Folie à Deux." Dreamlike sequences, blending reality and fantasy, required intricate choreography between actors and digital effects. These scenes were crafted to resemble the surreal, otherworldly quality of a musical dreamscape, with Arthur and his fellow characters moving through environments that shifted and morphed in response to the music.

Sound Design

The sound design was another layer of immersion, crafted to draw audiences into Arthur's world. The city's ambient noises—honking cars, distant sirens, murmuring crowds—were meticulously recorded and mixed to create a rich auditory backdrop. Dialogue was captured with a focus on naturalism, allowing the actors' performances to shine through.

The film's score, composed by Hildur Guðnadóttir, wove seamlessly into this sonic tapestry. Guðnadóttir's haunting, cello-driven themes from the first film were expanded upon, incorporating new musical motifs that reflected the film's deeper dive into shared madness. The integration of Lady Gaga's musical contributions added a fresh, dynamic element, with original songs that blended seamlessly into the narrative.

Challenges and Triumphs

Filming "Joker: Folie à Deux" was not without its challenges. The secrecy surrounding the plot and character developments required a level of logistical coordination that was both rigorous and exhaustive. Maintaining the integrity of the story while navigating public interest and media scrutiny demanded constant vigilance from the production team.

Weather posed another unpredictable element. Filming in New York and Chicago, cities known for their volatile climates, meant the production had to be adaptable. Sudden rainstorms, sweltering heat, and unexpected snowfalls all required adjustments to the shooting schedule and logistics. Yet these challenges often yielded serendipitous results, with natural weather conditions enhancing the film's atmosphere in ways that artificial effects could not replicate.

Chapter 2: The Cast and Characters
Joaquin Phoenix as Arthur Fleck/Joker

Joaquin Phoenix's embodiment of Arthur Fleck, who metamorphoses into the infamous Joker, stands as one of the most compelling portrayals in contemporary cinema. With "Joker: Folie à Deux," Phoenix delves even deeper into the psyche of this tormented character, bringing a level of intensity and nuance that is both unsettling and mesmerizing. His performance is a masterclass in method acting, showcasing his commitment to inhabiting the role in a way that blurs the line between actor and character.

The Preparation

Phoenix's preparation for the role of Arthur Fleck was nothing short of transformative. Known for his dedication to method acting, Phoenix immersed himself in the character's world long before the cameras started rolling. For the original "Joker," Phoenix lost a significant amount of weight to physically embody Arthur's emaciated, desperate state. This physical transformation was more than just a superficial change; it influenced his movement, his posture, and his overall presence on screen.

For "Folie à Deux," Phoenix underwent a similar regimen, shedding pounds to revisit Arthur's gaunt, fragile frame. However, this time, the transformation went beyond the physical. Phoenix spent months researching mental illness, diving into case studies and psychological texts to gain a deeper understanding of the conditions that plague Arthur. He also worked closely with psychiatrists and professionals who deal with similar cases, ensuring his portrayal was both respectful and accurate.

Phoenix's dedication extended to his emotional preparation as well. He isolated himself to explore the depths of Arthur's loneliness and alienation, often spending hours alone in his apartment, devoid of modern distractions. This self-imposed solitude allowed Phoenix to tap into the raw, unfiltered emotions that define Arthur's character, bringing an authenticity to his performance that resonates with audiences.

Performance Nuances

Phoenix's performance in "Folie à Deux" is a study in contrasts, capturing the duality of Arthur Fleck's existence. On one hand, there is the vulnerable, pitiable Arthur, a man who craves connection but is continually thwarted by a society that views him as an outcast. On the other, there is the Joker, a figure of anarchic liberation who revels in chaos and destruction. Phoenix navigates these extremes with a deftness that is both unsettling and compelling.

Body Language and Physicality

One of the most striking aspects of Phoenix's portrayal is his use of body language. Arthur's movements are jittery and awkward, reflecting his internal turmoil and lack of control. His hunched shoulders, downcast gaze, and hesitant gestures convey a sense of perpetual discomfort, as if he is never truly at ease in his own skin. In contrast, the Joker's physicality is fluid and confident, almost theatrical. His dance-like movements, which became iconic in the first film, are even more pronounced in "Folie à Deux," symbolizing his transformation from victim to villain.

Vocal Performance

Phoenix's vocal performance is another key element of his portrayal. Arthur's voice is soft and tentative, often cracking under the weight of his anxiety. His laugh, a disturbing, involuntary reaction to stress, is a tragic manifestation of his mental illness. The Joker's voice, however, is a chilling contrast—commanding, sardonic, and laced with dark humor. Phoenix modulates his tone to reflect the character's shifts in mood and sanity, creating a vocal landscape that is as unpredictable as it is haunting.

Emotional Depth

The emotional depth Phoenix brings to Arthur/Joker is perhaps the most compelling aspect of his performance. Every scene is layered with a complexity that invites the audience to empathize with Arthur's plight, even as they recoil from the Joker's actions. Phoenix portrays Arthur's pain and desperation with a raw honesty that is deeply affecting. His eyes, often brimming with tears or flickering with anger, convey a lifetime of suffering. When he transitions to the Joker, there is a terrifying clarity in his gaze—a look that suggests he has finally found his true self, no matter how twisted that self may be.

Impact on the Story

Phoenix's portrayal of Arthur Fleck/Joker is central to the narrative of "Folie à Deux." His character's journey from a marginalized outcast to a symbol of anarchy and madness drives the film's plot and themes. Arthur's interactions with the other characters, especially those who play pivotal roles in his transformation, are infused with tension and unpredictability.

The Arthur-Sophie Dynamic

One of the key relationships in the film is between Arthur and Sophie Dumond, played by Zazie Beetz. Their dynamic is fraught with complexity, as Sophie's initial sympathy for Arthur gradually turns to fear and revulsion as she witnesses his descent into madness. Phoenix and Beetz share a compelling on-screen chemistry that makes their scenes together particularly impactful. Arthur's yearning for Sophie's acceptance and the subsequent disillusionment when he realizes the impossibility of his desires adds a layer of tragic poignancy to his character arc.

Arthur's Relationship with Gotham

Arthur's interactions with the city of Gotham itself are also crucial. The city's indifference and hostility towards him reflect the larger societal issues of neglect and dehumanization.

Phoenix's performance captures the slow, simmering rage that builds within Arthur as he navigates the city's brutal streets and institutions. His ultimate transformation into the Joker is a direct response to the cruelty and alienation he experiences, making his actions both horrifying and, to some extent, understandable.

The Musical Dimension

"Folie à Deux" introduces a unique narrative element—musical sequences that delve into Arthur's psyche. Phoenix, alongside Lady Gaga, embraces this new dimension, blending performance art with character study. The musical numbers are not mere interludes but integral parts of the story, providing insight into Arthur's inner world. Phoenix's ability to transition seamlessly between intense dramatic moments and surreal musical sequences showcases his versatility and depth as an actor.

Lady Gaga's Role and Influence

When news broke that Lady Gaga would be joining Joaquin Phoenix in "Joker: Folie à Deux," the anticipation reached a fever pitch. Known for her transformative performances and fearless approach to her craft, Gaga's involvement signaled a new and intriguing direction for the sequel. Her role in the film is not just a testament to her versatility as an artist but also a crucial element in expanding the narrative of Arthur Fleck's descent into madness.

The Character

Lady Gaga takes on the role of Dr. Harleen Quinzel, a character who, in the annals of DC Comics lore, becomes the infamous Harley Quinn. Unlike previous iterations that leaned heavily into the whimsical and chaotic aspects of Harley Quinn, "Folie à Deux" reimagines her with a darker, more grounded approach. Dr. Quinzel is introduced as a psychiatrist at Arkham Asylum, where she encounters Arthur Fleck.

In "Folie à Deux," Dr. Quinzel is a complex character caught between professional duty and personal fascination. She begins as a compassionate and dedicated professional, intrigued by Arthur's case. As she delves deeper into his psyche, she finds herself drawn to his chaotic charm, leading to an intense and dangerous relationship. Gaga's portrayal is expected to bring a new depth to the character, exploring themes of obsession, mental illness, and the blurred lines between sanity and madness.

The Preparation

Lady Gaga is renowned for her immersive approach to her roles, and her preparation for Dr. Quinzel was no exception. Known for her commitment to authenticity, Gaga undertook a rigorous process to embody the character fully. She began by studying the origins and various interpretations of Harley Quinn, from her inception in the animated series to her comic book appearances and cinematic portrayals.

However, Gaga's preparation went beyond research. She consulted with psychologists and psychiatrists to understand the nuances of mental health, particularly the dynamics between a psychiatrist and a patient with complex, violent tendencies. This research was crucial in grounding her performance in reality, ensuring that her portrayal of Dr. Quinzel's transformation into Harley Quinn was both believable and poignant.

Gaga also engaged in method acting techniques, immersing herself in the character's emotional and psychological state. She spent time in psychiatric hospitals, observing interactions and therapies, to capture the authenticity of a professional deeply affected by her patient's condition. This dedication to understanding the character's professional world allowed Gaga to portray Dr. Quinzel's internal conflict with a nuanced and informed perspective.

The Performance

Gaga's performance in "Folie à Deux" is poised to be a revelation. Her ability to convey vulnerability and strength, coupled with her musical talents, adds layers to Dr. Quinzel's character. From her initial portrayal as a diligent and empathetic psychiatrist to her gradual descent into the chaotic allure of Arthur's world, Gaga's performance is expected to be both captivating and haunting.

Emotional Depth and Complexity

One of the standout aspects of Gaga's portrayal is her ability to convey the emotional complexity of Dr. Quinzel. Initially, she exudes professionalism and control, but as she becomes more entangled with Arthur, cracks begin to appear in her facade. Gaga's expressive eyes and subtle gestures communicate a wealth of emotions—curiosity, empathy, fear, and ultimately, a dangerous fascination. Her scenes with Phoenix are charged with intensity, as their characters' interactions oscillate between therapeutic sessions and increasingly personal encounters.

Musical Integration

A unique element of "Folie à Deux" is its incorporation of musical sequences, and Gaga's involvement elevates these moments. Known for her powerful voice and commanding stage presence, Gaga's musical performances within the film are not just interludes but integral parts of the narrative. These sequences delve into Dr. Quinzel's psyche, revealing her internal struggles and her growing infatuation with Arthur. The blend of dramatic acting and musical performance creates a surreal, dreamlike quality that enhances the film's exploration of madness and obsession.

Transformation into Harley Quinn

Gaga's transformation into Harley Quinn is expected to be a highlight of the film. This metamorphosis is portrayed not as a sudden shift but as a gradual, psychologically driven process. As Dr. Quinzel becomes more entangled in Arthur's world, her professional boundaries erode, and her fascination turns into a consuming obsession. Gaga's portrayal captures this descent with a combination of vulnerability and volatility, making the transition both tragic and inevitable.

Significance and Impact

Lady Gaga's role in "Folie à Deux" is significant for several reasons. Firstly, it represents a fresh take on a beloved character, offering audiences a deeper, more nuanced exploration of Harley Quinn's origins. By focusing on Dr. Quinzel's professional background and her psychological unraveling, the film provides a new lens through which to view her transformation.

Secondly, Gaga's performance adds a layer of gravitas and authenticity to the film. Her dedication to the role and her ability to convey complex emotions ensure that Dr. Quinzel's journey is both compelling and relatable. This portrayal challenges the traditional archetype of Harley Quinn, presenting her not merely as a sidekick or love interest but as a fully realized character with her own narrative arc.

Lastly, Gaga's musical contributions bring a unique dimension to the film. The integration of musical sequences allows for a more expressive and immersive exploration of the characters' inner worlds. These moments of musicality, juxtaposed with the film's darker themes, create a striking contrast that enhances the overall storytelling.

Supporting Cast and Their Characters

While Joaquin Phoenix and Lady Gaga take center stage in "Joker: Folie à Deux," the film's richness and depth are significantly enhanced by a stellar supporting cast. Each actor brings their unique flair and expertise, creating a tapestry of characters that deepen the narrative and provide a multifaceted view of Gotham's twisted world. Let's delve into the key supporting actors, their roles, and their contributions to the film's complex storyline.

Brendan Gleeson as Thomas Wayne

Brendan Gleeson, a seasoned actor known for his powerful presence and versatility, portrays Thomas Wayne. Unlike traditional depictions of Wayne as Gotham's philanthropic billionaire, Gleeson's interpretation offers a more morally ambiguous character. In "Folie à Deux," Thomas Wayne is depicted as a man whose wealth and influence have far-reaching consequences, some of which contribute to the societal decay seen through Arthur Fleck's eyes.

Gleeson's performance captures the duality of Wayne—a public figure striving for civic improvement while privately entangled in corruption and questionable decisions. His interactions with Arthur provide critical insights into the systemic issues plaguing Gotham, emphasizing the stark divide between the city's elite and its marginalized citizens. This nuanced portrayal challenges viewers to reconsider the character's legacy within the Batman mythos.

Catherine Keener as Dr. Eleanor Fitzmartin

Catherine Keener joins the cast as Dr. Eleanor Fitzmartin, a senior psychiatrist at Arkham Asylum. Keener's character serves as a mentor and foil to Dr. Harleen Quinzel, embodying the ethical and professional standards that Harleen gradually abandons. Dr. Fitzmartin's interactions with Arthur and Harleen are pivotal, highlighting the ethical dilemmas and psychological complexities inherent in their work.

Keener brings a blend of warmth and sternness to the role, making Dr. Fitzmartin a compelling figure who is both empathetic and authoritative. Her presence underscores the institutional challenges and moral quandaries faced by those working in mental health, particularly in an environment as grim as Arkham. Through her character, the film explores themes of professional integrity, the limitations of psychiatric care, and the fine line between empathy and manipulation.

Barry Keoghan as Charlie Dean

Barry Keoghan, an actor celebrated for his intense and often unsettling performances, portrays Charlie Dean, a fellow patient at Arkham Asylum. Dean is a character shrouded in mystery, his history and motivations slowly revealed through his interactions with Arthur and Harleen. Keoghan's portrayal adds an element of unpredictability and danger, as Dean's own descent into madness mirrors and contrasts with Arthur's transformation.

Keoghan's performance is marked by a chilling, almost otherworldly presence. His character serves as a catalyst for Arthur's further psychological unraveling, pushing him towards the brink of sanity. The dynamic between Dean and Arthur adds layers of tension and intrigue, showcasing the various manifestations of mental illness and the impact of institutionalization on individuals.

Zazie Beetz as Sophie Dumond

Returning from the first film, Zazie Beetz reprises her role as Sophie Dumond. In "Folie à Deux," Sophie's character is expanded, offering more depth and insight into her relationship with Arthur. Beetz's performance continues to blend vulnerability and strength, providing a humanizing counterpoint to Arthur's escalating madness.

In this sequel, Sophie is seen grappling with the aftermath

of her interactions with Arthur. Her character arc delves into themes of trauma, resilience, and the struggle to reclaim normalcy in the face of fear and chaos. Beetz's nuanced portrayal highlights Sophie's inner turmoil and determination, making her a relatable and sympathetic figure amidst the film's darker elements.

Frances Conroy as Penny Fleck

Frances Conroy returns as Penny Fleck, Arthur's deeply troubled mother. Conroy's portrayal in the first film was a haunting depiction of mental illness and its hereditary impact, and "Folie à Deux" continues to explore this theme. Penny's character serves as a reminder of Arthur's traumatic past and the deep-seated issues that have shaped his worldview.

Conroy's performance is both tragic and unsettling, capturing the complexities of a woman whose own mental health struggles have profoundly affected her son. Her interactions with Arthur provide critical context for his descent into madness, emphasizing the cyclical nature of trauma and the inescapable influence of familial bonds.

Brian Tyree Henry as Detective Carl Ford

Brian Tyree Henry joins the cast as Detective Carl Ford, a seasoned investigator tasked with unraveling the mysteries surrounding Arthur and the events at Arkham. Henry's character is portrayed as a diligent and morally upright figure, representing the law's often futile attempts to impose order on Gotham's chaos.

Detective Ford's pursuit of the truth brings him into direct conflict with Arthur and Harleen, creating a cat-and-mouse dynamic that adds tension and suspense to the narrative. Henry's performance balances determination with a sense of weariness, reflecting the challenges faced by those who seek justice in a city rife with corruption and disorder.

Sophie Okonedo as Mayor Vanessa Green

Sophie Okonedo plays Mayor Vanessa Green, Gotham's newly elected leader striving to implement reforms amidst the city's turmoil. Okonedo's portrayal captures the idealism and resolve of a politician determined to make a difference, despite the overwhelming odds and pervasive cynicism.

Mayor Green's interactions with Thomas Wayne and Detective Ford highlight the political and social dimensions of the story, providing a broader context for the individual struggles of the main characters. Okonedo's performance brings a sense of hope and urgency, emphasizing the importance of leadership and accountability in addressing systemic issues.

Jacob Tremblay as Young Arthur

Jacob Tremblay appears in flashbacks as young Arthur, providing glimpses into the formative experiences that have shaped his adult psyche. Tremblay's performance adds depth and poignancy to the character's backstory, illustrating the early signs of Arthur's psychological distress and the impact of his environment on his development.

These flashbacks are crucial in understanding Arthur's motivations and the origins of his fractured identity. Tremblay's portrayal is both heart-wrenching and illuminating, shedding light on the vulnerable child who would eventually become the Joker.

Chapter 3: Themes and Inspirations
Psychological Elements

"Joker: Folie à Deux" delves deeply into the psychological landscape of its characters, offering a rich tapestry of themes centered around mental health, identity, and society's impact on the individual. The film continues to explore the troubled psyche of Arthur Fleck while introducing new dimensions through the characters of Dr. Harleen Quinzel and others. Through its narrative, the film invites audiences to reflect on the complex interplay between the mind and the external world, examining how societal pressures and personal traumas shape and distort one's sense of self.

Mental Health

Arthur Fleck's Descent

At the heart of "Joker: Folie à Deux" is the exploration of Arthur Fleck's ongoing battle with mental illness. The first film introduced us to Arthur as a man grappling with delusions and uncontrollable bouts of laughter—a symptom of his underlying psychological disorders. In "Folie à Deux," we witness the further unraveling of his psyche as he descends deeper into madness. Arthur's journey is a stark representation of how untreated and misunderstood mental health issues can lead to catastrophic consequences.

The film portrays Arthur's mental health struggles with a raw and unflinching honesty. His hallucinations and delusions are depicted with a surreal, almost nightmarish quality, blurring the lines between reality and fantasy. These moments provide a window into Arthur's tormented mind, revealing the full extent of his detachment from reality. His interactions with the world around him are filtered through a lens of paranoia and delusion, making it difficult for the audience to discern what is real and what is imagined.

Dr. Harleen Quinzel's Transformation

The introduction of Dr. Harleen Quinzel adds another layer to the film's exploration of mental health. Initially presented as a competent and compassionate psychiatrist, Dr. Quinzel's descent into madness is both a personal tragedy and a reflection of the pervasive influence of Arthur's chaotic worldview. Her transformation into Harley Quinn is depicted as a gradual erosion of her professional boundaries and ethical standards, driven by her obsessive fascination with Arthur.

Dr. Quinzel's character arc serves as a cautionary tale about the dangers of becoming too personally involved with patients. Her initial empathy and desire to understand Arthur's condition become entangled with her own psychological vulnerabilities, leading to a profound identity crisis. The film examines how her professional detachment is compromised, ultimately resulting in her succumbing to the very madness she sought to cure. This descent is portrayed with a blend of horror and sympathy, highlighting the fragility of the human mind.

Identity

Arthur's Duality

Arthur Fleck's struggle with his identity is a central theme in "Folie à Deux." Throughout the film, he oscillates between his sense of self as a victimized outcast and his emerging identity as the Joker—a figure of anarchic liberation. This duality is explored through his interactions with other characters and the choices he makes in response to the world around him.

The Joker persona represents Arthur's attempt to reclaim control over his life and his environment. By embracing this new identity, he rejects the societal norms and expectations that have oppressed him. This transformation is depicted not as a simple switch but as a complex process fraught with internal conflict. Arthur's moments of self-awareness are interspersed with episodes of profound delusion, creating a character who is both deeply self-reflective and disturbingly unhinged.

Harleen Quinzel's Identity Crisis

Dr. Quinzel's transformation into Harley Quinn also involves a profound identity crisis. Her professional identity as a psychiatrist becomes increasingly untenable as she is drawn into Arthur's world. The film explores her internal struggle to maintain her sense of self while being seduced by the allure of Arthur's chaotic philosophy.

This crisis is depicted through her gradual adoption of the Harley Quinn persona—a mask that allows her to express her repressed desires and frustrations. The Harley Quinn identity becomes a means of escaping the constraints of her professional life and the societal expectations placed upon her as a woman in a male-dominated field. This transformation is portrayed with a blend of empowerment and tragedy, reflecting the complex dynamics of identity formation and dissolution.

Society's Impact on the Individual

Gotham as a Reflection of Societal Decay

The city of Gotham serves as a microcosm of societal decay and its impact on the individual. The film portrays Gotham as a place of stark economic disparity, rampant corruption, and pervasive violence. This environment acts as both a backdrop and a catalyst for the psychological breakdowns experienced by Arthur and Harleen.

Gotham's indifference and hostility towards its marginalized citizens are depicted through the harsh realities faced by the characters. Arthur's experiences of abuse, neglect, and social alienation are amplified by the city's systemic failures. The film uses Gotham to illustrate how societal structures and institutions can exacerbate mental health issues, pushing vulnerable individuals towards the brink of insanity.

The Role of Media and Public Perception

"Folie à Deux" also explores the role of media and public perception in shaping individual identities and mental health. Arthur's transformation into the Joker is both influenced by and influences the media's portrayal of him. The film critiques how sensationalist media can exploit and exacerbate personal tragedies for public consumption, creating a feedback loop of violence and notoriety.

Harleen's descent into madness is similarly influenced by her growing awareness of how she is perceived by others. Her interactions with the media and public opinion contribute to her identity crisis, highlighting the pressures faced by those in the public eye. The film examines the impact of external validation and condemnation on personal identity, emphasizing the destructive potential of societal scrutiny.

Thematic Depth and Narrative Complexity

"Joker: Folie à Deux" is a film rich in thematic depth, using its characters' psychological struggles to explore broader questions about human nature, societal norms, and the fragile boundaries of sanity. The narrative is layered with symbolic and metaphorical elements, creating a complex and thought-provoking tapestry that invites viewers to reflect on their own perceptions of reality and identity.

The Madness Within

One of the film's central themes is the idea that madness lies within all of us, waiting to be triggered by the right combination of external pressures and internal vulnerabilities. Arthur and Harleen's journeys are portrayed as extreme examples of what can happen when the delicate balance of the mind is disrupted. This theme is explored through their interactions with other characters, their responses to societal pressures, and their ultimate embrace of their darker selves.

The film suggests that madness is not a distant or foreign concept but an inherent part of the human experience. It challenges viewers to confront their own biases and assumptions about mental health, inviting them to consider the thin line that separates sanity from insanity.

The Search for Meaning

Another key theme is the search for meaning in a chaotic and indifferent world. Arthur and Harleen's transformations are driven by their desperate need to find purpose and identity in the face of overwhelming adversity. Their journeys reflect the human desire for significance and the lengths to which individuals will go to achieve it.

The film explores how this search for meaning can lead to both creative and destructive outcomes. Arthur's embrace of the Joker persona allows him to assert his identity and exert control over his environment, but it also leads to a path of violence and chaos. Harleen's transformation into Harley Quinn provides her with a sense of liberation and empowerment, but it also results in the loss of her professional integrity and personal stability.

Musical Influence and Themes

In "Joker: Folie à Deux," music plays a pivotal role, weaving through the narrative and accentuating the emotional depth of the story. The film's title itself, "Folie à Deux," hints at a symbiotic madness, a shared delusion, and this is mirrored in the haunting and evocative soundtrack. Music becomes a character in its own right, shaping the atmosphere and guiding the audience through the psychological labyrinths of Arthur Fleck and Dr. Harleen Quinzel. This chapter explores the intricate relationship between music and narrative in the film, delving into how the score and song choices enhance the storytelling.

The Score: A Symphony of Madness

Hildur Guðnadóttir's Return

Following her Oscar-winning score for the first "Joker" film, Hildur Guðnadóttir returns to craft the musical landscape of "Folie à Deux." Her compositions are renowned for their ability to evoke profound emotional responses, and her work on this sequel is no exception. Guðnadóttir's score is a haunting blend of orchestral and electronic elements, creating a soundscape that is both unsettling and mesmerizing.

The use of dissonant strings and melancholic melodies reflects Arthur's descent into madness and the pervasive sense of dread that permeates the film. Guðnadóttir's music captures the chaotic beauty of Arthur's transformation, oscillating between moments of quiet introspection and explosive crescendos that mirror his psychological state. Her compositions are layered with intricate details, inviting the audience to lose themselves in the music as much as in the narrative.

Leitmotifs and Character Themes

Guðnadóttir employs leitmotifs—recurring musical themes associated with specific characters or ideas—to deepen the audience's connection to the story. Arthur's theme, introduced in the first film, is revisited and expanded in "Folie à Deux." The haunting cello motif, which symbolizes his inner turmoil, is interwoven with new elements that reflect his evolving identity as the Joker.

Dr. Harleen Quinzel's transformation into Harley Quinn is accompanied by a distinct musical theme that evolves alongside her character. Initially, her theme is composed of delicate piano notes, reflecting her professionalism and empathy as a psychiatrist. As she becomes more entangled with Arthur and succumbs to her own madness, her theme shifts to incorporate discordant and frenetic elements, mirroring her descent into chaos.

Songs and Symbolism

Iconic Song Choices

In addition to Guðnadóttir's score, "Folie à Deux" features a carefully curated selection of songs that enhance the film's themes and emotional tone. These songs are not merely background music; they are integral to the storytelling, providing insight into the characters' minds and the world they inhabit.

One of the standout tracks is Frank Sinatra's "My Way," which plays during a pivotal moment in the film. The song's lyrics, reflecting a life lived on one's own terms, resonate deeply with Arthur's rejection of societal norms and his embrace of the Joker persona. Sinatra's smooth, confident voice juxtaposed with the chaos unfolding on screen creates a chillingly ironic contrast that underscores Arthur's twisted sense of liberation.

Lady Gaga's Musical Influence

Lady Gaga's involvement in the film extends beyond her acting role as Dr. Harleen Quinzel/Harley Quinn. Known for her powerful voice and theatrical flair, Gaga contributes original songs that serve as emotional touchstones within the narrative. Her musical influence is evident in several key scenes, where her songs encapsulate the intensity of her character's journey.

One such song, "Shattered Reflections," is a haunting ballad that plays during Harleen's moments of introspection and self-doubt. The lyrics, co-written by Gaga and Guðnadóttir, delve into themes of identity and transformation, capturing Harleen's internal struggle as she grapples with her attraction to Arthur and the darkness it awakens within her. Gaga's raw, emotive performance adds a visceral layer to the film, making her musical contributions an essential part of the storytelling.

Emotional Resonance

Creating Atmosphere

The music in "Folie à Deux" is instrumental in creating the film's atmosphere. The interplay between silence and sound heightens the tension and amplifies the emotional impact of each scene. Quiet, contemplative moments are punctuated by sudden bursts of music, reflecting the unpredictability of Arthur and Harleen's mental states.

In scenes where Arthur is alone, Guðnadóttir's sparse, haunting score underscores his isolation and inner turmoil. These moments are contrasted with scenes of frenetic activity, where the music becomes chaotic and overpowering, mirroring the external and internal chaos that defines Arthur's existence. The careful manipulation of musical dynamics draws the audience deeper into the characters' experiences, making their emotional journeys feel palpable and immediate.

Enhancing Character Development

Music also plays a crucial role in character development. Arthur's dance sequences, set to Guðnadóttir's evocative score, serve as a window into his psyche. These dances, both unsettling and strangely beautiful, are moments of catharsis for Arthur, where he feels a sense of freedom and control. The music in these scenes captures the duality of his character—both victim and villain, fragile and fierce.

For Harleen, music becomes a means of expression as she transitions into Harley Quinn. Gaga's songs, with their intense emotion and dramatic flair, reflect Harleen's internal struggle and eventual embrace of her new identity. The shift in her musical theme from soft piano to bold, dramatic orchestration mirrors her transformation from a composed psychiatrist to a chaotic and unpredictable force.

Musical Techniques and Innovations

Sound Design

"Folie à Deux" employs innovative sound design techniques to enhance the film's psychological themes. The blending of diegetic and non-diegetic sounds blurs the line between reality and Arthur's perception of it. For instance, the sound of a ticking clock may seamlessly transition into a rhythmic element of the score, creating a sense of disorientation and unease.

The use of soundscapes—ambient noises that reflect the environment—adds another layer of immersion. The sounds of Gotham's bustling streets, the creaking of old buildings, and the whispers of distant conversations all contribute to the film's gritty, oppressive atmosphere. These elements, combined with the score, create a rich auditory experience that pulls the audience into the world of the film.

Musical Symbolism

The film's musical symbolism is also noteworthy. Specific instruments and musical motifs are used to represent different aspects of the characters' psyches. For example, the cello, with its deep, resonant tones, is associated with Arthur's melancholic and contemplative moments, while the use of dissonant strings and percussion highlights his descent into madness.

Harleen's musical journey is marked by the piano, an instrument that starts as a symbol of her professional identity and composure. As her character evolves, the piano's melodies become more complex and discordant, reflecting her internal conflict and eventual transformation. This musical symbolism adds depth to the narrative, providing a non-verbal means of exploring the characters' inner worlds.

Connection to the First Joker Movie

"Joker: Folie à Deux" continues the story of Arthur Fleck, diving deeper into the character's psyche and expanding on the themes introduced in the first "Joker" movie. Directed by Todd Phillips, both films offer a gritty and introspective look at the transformation of Arthur Fleck into the iconic Joker. This chapter explores the connections between the two films, highlighting narrative continuities, thematic parallels, and character development, all while maintaining an engaging and analytical tone.

Narrative Continuities

Arthur Fleck's Journey

The narrative of "Joker: Folie à Deux" picks up where the first film left off, with Arthur Fleck fully embracing his identity as the Joker. The first movie ends with Arthur standing triumphant on a police car, basking in the chaos he has incited. "Folie à Deux" delves into the aftermath of this moment, exploring how Arthur navigates his new identity and the consequences of his actions.

One of the key continuities is Arthur's struggle with his mental health. The first film depicted his descent into madness, driven by societal neglect and personal trauma. "Folie à Deux" continues to explore this theme, examining how Arthur's mental state evolves now that he has embraced his alter ego. His interactions with Dr. Harleen Quinzel add a new dimension to this exploration, as her own psychological journey becomes intertwined with his.

Setting and Atmosphere

Gotham City remains a central element in both films, serving as a backdrop that reflects the chaos and decay of Arthur's mind. The first "Joker" movie painted a bleak picture of Gotham, rife with crime, poverty, and corruption. "Folie à Deux" continues to portray the city in a similar light, emphasizing its role in shaping the characters' psyches.

The visual and auditory aesthetics of the first film are carried over into the sequel, creating a cohesive cinematic universe. The oppressive atmosphere, characterized by dim lighting, claustrophobic spaces, and a haunting score, is maintained in "Folie à Deux," ensuring that the audience remains immersed in the dark world that Arthur inhabits.

Thematic Parallels

Mental Health and Society

Both "Joker" films are deeply concerned with the theme of mental health and its intersection with societal issues. The first movie highlighted the neglect and stigmatization faced by those with mental illnesses, as seen through Arthur's struggles to access care and support. "Folie à Deux" expands on this theme by introducing Dr. Harleen Quinzel, whose professional role as a psychiatrist contrasts sharply with her eventual descent into madness.

The theme of society's impact on individual mental health is explored through Harleen's transformation. Her initial empathy and desire to help Arthur are gradually eroded by the systemic failures and personal traumas she encounters. This parallel narrative underscores the idea that mental illness is not just an individual issue but a societal one, exacerbated by neglect and abuse.

Identity and Transformation

The exploration of identity is a central theme in both films. In the first "Joker" movie, Arthur's transformation into the Joker is depicted as a tragic and violent assertion of his identity in response to a hostile world. "Folie à Deux" continues this exploration, focusing on how Arthur and Harleen grapple with their evolving identities.

Arthur's duality—his struggle between his sense of self and his Joker persona—remains a focal point. The sequel delves deeper into this conflict, examining how Arthur navigates the boundaries between his identities. Harleen's transformation into Harley Quinn mirrors Arthur's journey, highlighting the fluid and often destructive nature of identity formation in the face of external pressures.

Character Development

Arthur Fleck/Joker

Joaquin Phoenix's portrayal of Arthur Fleck/Joker is central to both films, offering a nuanced and deeply unsettling depiction of a man driven to the brink by his circumstances. In the first movie, Arthur's character arc is defined by his descent into madness and his ultimate embrace of the Joker persona. "Folie à Deux" continues to develop this character, exploring the complexities of his new identity.

In the sequel, Arthur's character is further fleshed out as he navigates his newfound power and notoriety. His interactions with Harleen Quinzel provide insight into his manipulative and charismatic aspects, revealing how he draws others into his world. Phoenix's performance continues to capture the multifaceted nature of Arthur, balancing vulnerability and menace in a way that keeps the audience both empathetic and horrified.

Harleen Quinzel/Harley Quinn

The introduction of Lady Gaga as Dr. Harleen Quinzel adds a new layer to the character dynamics in "Folie à Deux." Harleen's journey from a compassionate psychiatrist to the chaotic and unpredictable Harley Quinn is a central narrative thread in the sequel. Her character development is intricately linked to Arthur's, creating a complex and symbiotic relationship.

Harleen's transformation is depicted with a mix of tragedy and inevitability. Her initial professional detachment and empathy gradually give way to obsession and madness as she becomes more entangled with Arthur. This development mirrors Arthur's own journey, highlighting the film's exploration of how close relationships can both heal and destroy.

Symbolic and Visual Connections

Iconic Imagery

Both "Joker" films are rich with symbolic imagery that enhances their thematic depth. The use of mirrors, for instance, is a recurring motif that symbolizes the characters' introspection and identity struggles. In the first film, Arthur's frequent encounters with mirrors reflect his fragmented sense of self. "Folie à Deux" continues this visual symbolism, using mirrors to depict Harleen's gradual loss of identity and her merging with the Harley Quinn persona.

Another iconic image carried over from the first film is the Joker's dance. Arthur's dance sequences, set to Hildur Guðnadóttir's haunting score, are moments of catharsis and transformation. In "Folie à Deux," these dances become a shared ritual between Arthur and Harleen, symbolizing their shared descent into madness and their rejection of societal norms.

The Clown Mask

The clown mask, an emblem of Arthur's Joker persona, remains a powerful symbol in the sequel. In the first film, the mask represents Arthur's transformation and his rebellion against a society that has marginalized and abused him. In "Folie à Deux," the mask takes on new significance as it becomes a shared symbol between Arthur and Harleen.

The film explores how the mask allows both characters to hide their true selves and embrace their chaotic identities. The mask's symbolism is deepened by its association with anonymity and liberation, highlighting the characters' desire to escape societal constraints and express their true natures.

Chapter 4: Behind the Scenes
Director Todd Phillips' Vision

Todd Phillips, the visionary director behind the first "Joker" movie, returns to helm "Joker: Folie à Deux," bringing his unique blend of dark humor, gritty realism, and psychological depth to the sequel. His approach to filmmaking, deeply rooted in his passion for character-driven narratives and his fascination with the human psyche, shapes every frame of the film. This chapter delves into Phillips' creative vision for "Folie à Deux," exploring his inspirations, directorial style, and the innovative techniques he employs to bring this compelling story to life.

Creative Approach

Expanding the Universe

Phillips' vision for "Folie à Deux" was to expand the universe established in the first film, delving deeper into the complexities of Arthur Fleck's character while introducing new elements that enrich the narrative. Unlike many sequels that simply extend the storyline, Phillips sought to create a film that stands on its own, offering a fresh perspective on the Joker mythos while maintaining continuity with its predecessor.

To achieve this, Phillips focused on the psychological and emotional landscapes of his characters. He aimed to explore not just the outward manifestations of their madness but the inner turmoil and societal pressures that drive them. This deeper exploration required a nuanced approach to storytelling, one that balances the darkness of the Joker's world with moments of unexpected tenderness and humanity.

Collaboration with Writers and Actors

Central to Phillips' creative process is his collaboration with writers and actors. For "Folie à Deux," he worked closely with co-writer Scott Silver, with whom he penned the first "Joker" movie. Together, they crafted a screenplay that delves into the symbiotic relationship between Arthur Fleck and Dr. Harleen Quinzel, exploring themes of madness, identity, and the fine line between sanity and insanity.

Phillips is known for his collaborative approach with actors, encouraging them to bring their own interpretations and insights to their characters. Joaquin Phoenix's transformative performance in the first film was a result of this synergy, and Phillips continued this collaborative spirit in the sequel. He worked intensively with Phoenix and Lady Gaga, creating an environment where they could explore and inhabit their roles fully, resulting in performances that are both deeply personal and universally resonant.

Inspirations

Cinematic Influences

Phillips' vision for "Folie à Deux" is informed by a rich tapestry of cinematic influences. He draws inspiration from classic films that explore themes of madness and societal alienation, such as Martin Scorsese's "Taxi Driver" and "The King of Comedy." These films, with their gritty realism and complex character studies, provide a blueprint for Phillips' own approach to storytelling.

Another significant influence is Stanley Kubrick, particularly his use of visual symbolism and his ability to create immersive, unsettling atmospheres. Phillips employs similar techniques in "Folie à Deux," using stark imagery and meticulous attention to detail to evoke the psychological states of his characters. The result is a film that is visually striking and emotionally intense, drawing the audience into the inner worlds of Arthur and Harleen.

Musical Inspirations

Music plays a crucial role in Phillips' vision for "Folie à Deux," both as a narrative device and as an emotional undercurrent. He was inspired by the way music can enhance storytelling, creating a symbiotic relationship between the score and the narrative. This inspiration is evident in his collaboration with composer Hildur Guðnadóttir, whose haunting score for the first "Joker" film set a new standard for cinematic music.

Phillips also drew inspiration from Lady Gaga's musical artistry. Her ability to convey deep emotion through her music informed her character's journey and the overall tone of the film. By integrating music into the fabric of the narrative, Phillips created a film that resonates on multiple sensory levels, using sound to amplify the emotional and psychological impact of the story.

Directorial Style

Visual Storytelling

Phillips' directorial style is characterized by his emphasis on visual storytelling. He uses every element within the frame to convey meaning, from the composition and lighting to the color palette and set design. This meticulous attention to detail creates a visually cohesive and immersive world that reflects the inner states of the characters.

In "Folie à Deux," Phillips employs a muted color palette, dominated by grays, blacks, and deep reds, to evoke the bleakness and violence of Gotham City. The stark contrast between light and shadow highlights the duality of Arthur and Harleen's characters, underscoring their internal conflicts. This visual approach is complemented by the film's production design, which creates a sense of claustrophobia and decay, mirroring the characters' psychological entrapment.

Cinematography and Editing

Phillips works closely with his cinematographer, Lawrence Sher, to achieve a specific visual aesthetic that enhances the narrative. In "Folie à Deux," the camera movements are deliberate and often intimate, capturing the subtleties of the characters' expressions and movements. Close-up shots are used to emphasize moments of emotional intensity, while wider shots depict the vast, oppressive environment of Gotham.

The editing, handled by Jeff Groth, reflects Phillips' desire to create a seamless and immersive narrative flow. The pacing of "Folie à Deux" is carefully calibrated to build tension and release it in moments of heightened drama. Groth's editing style ensures that the audience remains engaged, drawing them deeper into the story with each scene.

Innovative Techniques

Immersive Sound Design

Phillips' innovative use of sound design enhances the immersive quality of "Folie à Deux." He collaborates with sound designers to create a rich auditory landscape that reflects the psychological states of the characters. The use of diegetic and non-diegetic sounds blurs the line between reality and illusion, drawing the audience into Arthur and Harleen's fragmented perceptions.

One notable technique is the integration of ambient sounds with the musical score. The sounds of Gotham—sirens, distant conversations, the hum of the city—are woven into the music, creating a seamless auditory experience. This technique not only grounds the audience in the film's setting but also heightens the sense of unease and disorientation that pervades the narrative.

Experimental Filming Methods

Phillips is known for his willingness to experiment with filming methods to achieve a specific artistic vision. In "Folie à Deux," he employs a variety of techniques to convey the characters' psychological states. For instance, he uses handheld cameras to create a sense of immediacy and instability, reflecting the characters' inner turmoil. This technique contrasts with the more controlled, static shots that depict moments of calm or reflection, highlighting the volatility of Arthur and Harleen's worlds.

Additionally, Phillips experiments with lighting and color to evoke specific emotions. The use of chiaroscuro lighting—strong contrasts between light and dark—creates a sense of depth and drama, emphasizing the duality and conflict within the characters. Color is used symbolically, with certain hues associated with key moments or themes, guiding the audience's emotional responses.

Phillips' Artistic Vision

Emphasizing Character Complexity

A hallmark of Phillips' vision is his focus on character complexity. He is drawn to flawed, multifaceted characters whose struggles and transformations resonate on a human level. In "Folie à Deux," this approach is evident in the nuanced portrayals of Arthur and Harleen, whose journeys are marked by ambiguity and moral complexity.

Phillips emphasizes the humanity of his characters, even as they descend into madness and violence. He explores their vulnerabilities, motivations, and relationships, creating a sense of empathy and understanding. This focus on character complexity ensures that "Folie à Deux" is not just a story about villains but a profound exploration of the human condition.

Blurring Genre Boundaries

Phillips' vision for "Folie à Deux" involves blurring the boundaries between genres, creating a film that defies easy categorization. While the first "Joker" movie was a character study with elements of psychological thriller and drama, the sequel incorporates additional layers, including musical elements and dark comedy.

This genre-blending approach reflects Phillips' belief that storytelling should be dynamic and multifaceted. By combining different genres, he creates a richer, more textured narrative that challenges audience expectations and deepens their engagement with the film. The musical sequences, in particular, add a new dimension to the story, using song and dance to express the characters' emotions in a visceral and theatrical way.

Screenwriting and Story Development

The process of crafting the screenplay for "Joker: Folie à Deux" was a journey as complex and multifaceted as the characters it sought to portray. With the immense success and critical acclaim of the first "Joker" film, expectations were high for its sequel. The task of meeting these expectations fell to the dynamic writing duo of Todd Phillips and Scott Silver, who aimed to create a story that was both a continuation and an evolution of Arthur Fleck's tumultuous journey. This chapter delves into the intricacies of the screenwriting and story development process, exploring the writing team, key story arcs, and notable changes during development.

The Writing Team

Todd Phillips and Scott Silver

Todd Phillips, known for his distinct blend of dark humor and character-driven narratives, teamed up once again with Scott Silver, a screenwriter renowned for his ability to weave complex, emotionally resonant stories. Their collaboration on the first "Joker" movie resulted in a screenplay that was both harrowing and poignant, earning them an Academy Award nomination for Best Adapted Screenplay.

For "Folie à Deux," Phillips and Silver sought to deepen their exploration of the Joker's psyche while introducing new characters and themes. Their writing process was characterized by intense brainstorming sessions, during which they delved into the psychological and emotional depths of their characters. They aimed to create a story that was not only a sequel but a standalone narrative with its own unique identity.

Lady Gaga's Contribution

In an interesting turn of events, Lady Gaga, who plays Dr. Harleen Quinzel/Harley Quinn in the film, also contributed to the screenplay development. Known for her multifaceted artistic talents, Gaga brought a fresh perspective to the story, particularly in shaping her character's arc. Her insights into Harleen's transformation added depth and nuance to the screenplay, ensuring that the character's journey was both compelling and authentic.

Key Story Arcs

Arthur Fleck's Continued Descent

The primary narrative arc of "Folie à Deux" continues the story of Arthur Fleck, who has fully embraced his identity as the Joker. The screenplay explores the consequences of his actions at the end of the first film, where he incited chaos and violence in Gotham City. Arthur's journey in the sequel is marked by his struggle to maintain control over his alter ego while grappling with the increasing notoriety and influence of the Joker persona.

Phillips and Silver aimed to depict Arthur's psychological decline in a manner that was both believable and harrowing. The screenplay delves into his interactions with society, his relationship with Harleen Quinzel, and his internal conflicts. These elements combine to create a complex character study that reflects the duality and turmoil within Arthur's mind.

The Transformation of Harleen Quinzel

A significant focus of the screenplay is the transformation of Dr. Harleen Quinzel into Harley Quinn. Harleen starts as a compassionate and dedicated psychiatrist assigned to Arthur's case. Her initial interactions with Arthur are professional, driven by a desire to understand and help him. However, as she becomes more entangled in his world, her own mental state begins to unravel.

Phillips and Silver crafted Harleen's arc to mirror and contrast Arthur's journey. While Arthur's transformation is characterized by an externalization of his madness, Harleen's descent is more insidious, marked by a gradual erosion of her identity and morals. The screenplay explores the factors that contribute to her transformation, including her personal traumas, her fascination with Arthur, and the systemic failures of the mental health system.

Thematic Exploration

The screenplay of "Folie à Deux" continues to explore the themes of mental health, societal neglect, and the fine line between sanity and insanity. Phillips and Silver aimed to create a narrative that was not just a continuation of the first film but a deeper exploration of these themes. The story examines how individuals are shaped by their environments and how societal failures can drive people to the brink of madness.

One of the key thematic arcs is the idea of folie à deux, a psychological phenomenon where two individuals share a delusion. This theme is central to the relationship between Arthur and Harleen, highlighting how their interactions exacerbate each other's mental instability. The screenplay uses this concept to explore the dynamics of their relationship and the mutual descent into chaos.

Notable Changes During Development

Evolving the Script

The development of "Folie à Deux" was marked by several notable changes as Phillips and Silver refined the screenplay. Initially, the sequel was envisioned as a direct continuation of the first film, focusing primarily on Arthur's journey. However, as the writing process progressed, the character of Harleen Quinzel became more central to the narrative.

Phillips and Silver decided to expand Harleen's role, making her transformation into Harley Quinn a core element of the story. This shift required significant rewrites to ensure that her arc was fully developed and integrated into the overall narrative. The decision to cast Lady Gaga, with her unique artistic vision, further influenced the evolution of Harleen's character and the screenplay.

Integrating Musical Elements

A unique aspect of "Folie à Deux" is its integration of musical elements, a departure from the first film's more grounded approach. This decision was influenced by Lady Gaga's involvement and Phillips' desire to experiment with genre-blending. The screenplay incorporates several musical sequences that serve as both narrative and emotional expressions of the characters' inner worlds.

These musical elements required careful development to ensure they were seamlessly integrated into the story. Phillips and Silver worked closely with Gaga and the film's musical team to create sequences that were both visually and thematically cohesive. The result is a screenplay that uses music to enhance the narrative, providing a deeper insight into the characters' psyches.

Crafting the Dialogue

Character-Driven Dialogue

Phillips and Silver's approach to dialogue in "Folie à Deux" was character-driven, aiming to capture the unique voices of Arthur and Harleen. Arthur's dialogue reflects his fragmented psyche and his struggle to articulate his thoughts and emotions. His interactions with Harleen are marked by a mix of vulnerability and manipulation, revealing the complexities of their relationship.

Harleen's dialogue evolves over the course of the screenplay, mirroring her transformation. Initially, her speech is professional and empathetic, reflecting her role as a psychiatrist. As she becomes more entangled with Arthur, her dialogue takes on a more chaotic and emotional tone, highlighting her descent into madness. This evolution required careful crafting to ensure it felt natural and believable.

Balancing Exposition and Subtext

One of the challenges in writing the screenplay was balancing exposition with subtext. Phillips and Silver aimed to convey key plot points and character motivations without resorting to overt exposition. Instead, they used subtext and visual storytelling to communicate the underlying themes and emotions.

For example, the theme of folie à deux is conveyed through the characters' interactions and shared experiences, rather than explicit dialogue. Similarly, the societal neglect and failures that drive Arthur and Harleen's transformations are depicted through their environments and the systemic obstacles they face. This approach ensures that the screenplay remains engaging and thought-provoking, encouraging the audience to infer meaning from the characters' actions and surroundings.

Cinematography and Visual Style

"Joker: Folie à Deux" continues the tradition of its predecessor by immersing the audience in a visually rich and emotionally intense cinematic experience. The film's cinematography and visual style, crafted under the expert eye of director Todd Phillips and cinematographer Lawrence Sher, play a crucial role in bringing the story to life. Every frame is meticulously designed to reflect the characters' psychological states and the bleak, chaotic world of Gotham City. This chapter delves into the techniques, color schemes, and visual motifs used to tell the story of "Joker: Folie à Deux," offering a vivid and immersive look at the film's visual approach.

Techniques

Cinematography by Lawrence Sher

Lawrence Sher, who also worked on the first "Joker" film, returns as the cinematographer for "Folie à Deux." His collaboration with Todd Phillips has resulted in a visual style that is both cohesive and innovative, enhancing the narrative through carefully crafted imagery. Sher's approach to cinematography in the sequel is characterized by a blend of traditional techniques and experimental methods, creating a film that is visually striking and emotionally resonant.

Handheld Camera Work: One of the defining techniques used in "Folie à Deux" is the extensive use of handheld camera work. This approach adds a sense of immediacy and intimacy, drawing the audience into the characters' personal spaces. The handheld shots are particularly effective in capturing the chaotic and unstable nature of Arthur Fleck's world, as well as the burgeoning relationship between Arthur and Harleen Quinzel. The subtle shake and movement of the camera mirror the internal turmoil of the characters, making their experiences more visceral for the viewer.

Steadicam Shots: In contrast to the handheld camera work,

Sher employs Steadicam shots to provide moments of clarity and stability within the film. These shots are often used to highlight key moments of introspection or revelation, allowing the audience to focus on the emotional depth of the characters. The smooth, fluid movement of the Steadicam creates a sense of calm and control, juxtaposed against the otherwise chaotic visual style.

Close-Ups and Extreme Close-Ups: Close-ups and extreme close-ups are used extensively to capture the nuanced performances of Joaquin Phoenix and Lady Gaga. These shots allow the audience to see every flicker of emotion and every subtle change in expression, providing a window into the characters' inner worlds. The intensity of these close-ups underscores the psychological depth of the film, making the characters' experiences more immediate and relatable.

Color Schemes

The Palette of Madness

The color scheme of "Joker: Folie à Deux" is a crucial element in conveying the film's themes and mood. Phillips and Sher use a carefully curated palette to reflect the psychological states of the characters and the oppressive atmosphere of Gotham City.

Muted Colors: The overall color palette of the film is dominated by muted tones, including grays, blacks, and browns. These colors evoke a sense of bleakness and despair, mirroring the characters' internal struggles and the decaying environment of Gotham. The muted palette creates a stark contrast with the occasional bursts of color, highlighting moments of significance and emotional intensity.

Symbolic Use of Color: Color is used symbolically throughout the film to underscore key themes and character dynamics. For example, the color red is often associated with moments of violence and transformation, representing both danger and empowerment. Arthur's Joker persona is frequently linked with shades of red, emphasizing his shift from victim to villain. In contrast, Harleen Quinzel's transformation into Harley Quinn is marked by a transition from soft, pastel colors to more vibrant and chaotic hues, reflecting her descent into madness.

Chiaroscuro Lighting: The use of chiaroscuro lighting—strong contrasts between light and dark—is another hallmark of the film's visual style. This technique creates a sense of depth and drama, highlighting the duality and conflict within the characters. The interplay of light and shadow not only enhances the film's visual appeal but also serves to underscore the themes of sanity and insanity, good and evil.

Visual Motifs

Reflections and Mirrors

Reflections and mirrors are recurring visual motifs in "Joker: Folie à Deux," symbolizing the fractured identities and duality of the characters. These motifs are used to explore the themes of self-perception and transformation, adding a layer of complexity to the visual narrative.

Mirrors as a Symbol of Duality: Mirrors often appear in scenes where characters are grappling with their identities or undergoing significant changes. For instance, Arthur's frequent gazes into mirrors reflect his internal struggle and his evolving Joker persona. Similarly, Harleen's interactions with mirrors underscore her psychological descent and the blurring of her professional and personal boundaries.

Distorted Reflections: Distorted reflections are used to convey the characters' fragmented perceptions and the instability of their mental states. These reflections appear in various forms, such as warped mirrors, reflective surfaces, and even water. The distortion of these images mirrors the characters' sense of disorientation and their tenuous grasp on reality, enhancing the film's psychological tension.

Set Design and Production

The World of Gotham City

The set design and production of "Joker: Folie à Deux" play a pivotal role in creating the immersive and oppressive atmosphere of Gotham City. The city itself is a character in the film, its decaying infrastructure and gritty streets reflecting the societal decay and moral corruption that permeate the narrative.

Urban Decay: The depiction of urban decay is a central element of the film's visual style. The sets are designed to evoke a sense of neglect and deterioration, with crumbling buildings, graffiti-covered walls, and litter-strewn streets. This environment not only provides a realistic backdrop for the story but also symbolizes the systemic failures and societal neglect that drive the characters to the brink of madness.

Claustrophobic Interiors: The interiors of the film, particularly those associated with Arthur and Harleen, are designed to be claustrophobic and confining. The cramped, dimly lit spaces reflect the characters' sense of entrapment and isolation, both physically and psychologically. The use of tight framing and limited space heightens the sense of tension and unease, drawing the audience into the characters' claustrophobic worlds.

Contrasting Spaces: The film also uses contrasting spaces to highlight the characters' emotional and psychological journeys. For example, Arthur's apartment is depicted as dark and cluttered, symbolizing his chaotic mind, while Harleen's office is initially portrayed as orderly and professional. As the story progresses and Harleen's transformation unfolds, her environment becomes increasingly disordered, mirroring her internal turmoil.

Innovative Visual Techniques

Experimental Camera Angles

Phillips and Sher employ a variety of experimental camera angles to enhance the film's visual storytelling and convey the characters' psychological states.

Dutch Angles: Dutch angles, where the camera is tilted to create a sense of unease, are used throughout the film to reflect the characters' instability and the chaotic nature of their world. These angles distort the viewer's perspective, creating a disorienting effect that mirrors the characters' mental states.

Extreme Close-Ups and Wide Shots: The film juxtaposes extreme close-ups with wide shots to create a dynamic visual experience. Close-ups are used to capture the intense emotions and inner turmoil of the characters, while wide shots depict the vast, oppressive environment of Gotham City. This contrast emphasizes the characters' isolation and vulnerability within the larger, indifferent world.

Point-of-View Shots: Point-of-view shots are employed to immerse the audience in the characters' experiences, allowing them to see the world through Arthur and Harleen's eyes. These shots enhance the psychological depth of the film, creating a sense of empathy and connection with the characters' struggles.

Visual Symbolism

Masks and Makeup

Masks and makeup are powerful visual symbols in "Joker: Folie à Deux," representing the characters' attempts to hide their true selves and the personas they adopt to navigate their world.

Arthur's Joker Makeup: Arthur's Joker makeup is a central visual motif, symbolizing his transformation from a marginalized individual to a figure of chaos and rebellion. The makeup serves as both a mask and a form of self-expression, reflecting his internal conflict and his desire to be seen and acknowledged. The act of applying the makeup is depicted as a ritualistic process, emphasizing its significance in Arthur's identity.

Harleen's Transformation: Harleen's journey to becoming Harley Quinn is marked by her adoption of makeup and costumes that reflect her evolving identity. Her transformation is visually represented through changes in her appearance, from her initial professional demeanor to her final, chaotic persona. The makeup and costumes serve as visual markers of her descent into madness, highlighting the performative aspects of her new identity.

Chapter 5: Music and Soundtrack
Composers and Key Tracks

Music plays a pivotal role in shaping the atmosphere and emotional landscape of a film, and "Joker: Folie à Deux" is no exception. The sequel builds on the haunting and evocative soundtrack of the first film, introducing new compositions and themes that deepen the narrative and enrich the viewing experience. This chapter delves into the backgrounds of the composers, the creative process behind the soundtrack, and the significance of key tracks that punctuate the film's most memorable moments.

The Composers

Hildur Guðnadóttir: Returning Maestro

Hildur Guðnadóttir, the Icelandic composer who garnered critical acclaim for her work on the original "Joker" film, returns to score "Folie à Deux." Her innovative use of cello, voice, and electronic elements in the first film's soundtrack earned her an Academy Award, a Grammy, and a Golden Globe. Guðnadóttir's music is known for its ability to convey deep emotional resonance and psychological complexity, making her an ideal choice to continue the musical journey of Arthur Fleck.

Background: Guðnadóttir's background in classical music and her experience with avant-garde and experimental compositions have shaped her distinctive sound. Her early work with artists like Jóhann Jóhannsson and her solo projects reflect a profound understanding of how music can evoke and manipulate emotion.

Approach: For "Folie à Deux," Guðnadóttir expands on the themes she introduced in the first film, while exploring new sonic landscapes that reflect the evolving narrative. Her approach involves blending traditional orchestral elements with innovative sound design, creating a soundtrack that is both timeless and contemporary.

Lady Gaga: A New Voice

In a bold and inspired move, Lady Gaga, who also stars as Harleen Quinzel/Harley Quinn, contributes to the soundtrack. Known for her powerful vocals and genre-spanning musical talents, Gaga brings a fresh and dynamic energy to the film's music.

Background: Lady Gaga's career is marked by her versatility and ability to reinvent herself across various musical styles, from pop and rock to jazz and classical. Her work on "A Star Is Born" showcased her ability to convey deep emotion through music, making her a fitting addition to the "Folie à Deux" soundtrack.

Contribution: Gaga's involvement in the soundtrack goes beyond her performance in the film. She has co-composed several key tracks, lending her unique voice and creative vision to the project. Her contributions add a new dimension to the soundtrack, enhancing the emotional depth and complexity of the film's music.

The Creation Process

Collaborative Synergy

The creation of the "Folie à Deux" soundtrack was a deeply collaborative process, with Guðnadóttir and Gaga working closely with director Todd Phillips to ensure the music aligns seamlessly with the film's narrative and visual style.

Integration with Narrative: Phillips emphasized the importance of music in conveying the psychological states of the characters and the overarching themes of the film. The composers were involved from the early stages of production, allowing them to develop musical themes that are intricately woven into the story.

Innovative Techniques: The creative process involved the use of unconventional recording techniques and experimental sound design. Guðnadóttir's innovative use of cello and electronic elements is complemented by Gaga's powerful vocal performances, resulting in a soundtrack that is both haunting and mesmerizing.

Recording Sessions

The recording sessions for the soundtrack took place in a variety of settings, from traditional studios to more unconventional locations that provided unique acoustic qualities.

Live Orchestration: Key tracks feature live orchestration, with Guðnadóttir conducting a full orchestra to capture the grandeur and intensity of the film's emotional peaks. The use of live instruments adds a richness and depth to the soundtrack, creating a powerful auditory experience.

Intimate Vocals: Gaga's vocal tracks were recorded in intimate settings, capturing the raw emotion and vulnerability of her character. These recordings are interspersed with the orchestral pieces, creating a dynamic interplay between the two musical styles.

Key Tracks

"Harlequin's Lament"

One of the standout tracks on the "Folie à Deux" soundtrack is "Harlequin's Lament," a hauntingly beautiful piece that encapsulates the emotional journey of Harleen Quinzel as she transforms into Harley Quinn.

Musical Composition: The track begins with a delicate piano melody, gradually building with the addition of strings and electronic elements. Gaga's vocals enter softly, growing in intensity as the song progresses. The orchestration swells to a crescendo, reflecting the character's inner turmoil and eventual acceptance of her new identity.

Significance: "Harlequin's Lament" serves as a musical centerpiece for the film, capturing the essence of Harleen's transformation. The combination of Guðnadóttir's evocative composition and Gaga's powerful performance creates a deeply moving and unforgettable musical experience.

"The Joker's Waltz"

Another key track is "The Joker's Waltz," which serves as a leitmotif for Arthur Fleck's descent into madness and his embrace of the Joker persona.

Musical Composition: The waltz is characterized by its unsettling, off-kilter rhythm and dissonant harmonies. The use of a traditional waltz form juxtaposed with eerie, discordant elements creates a sense of unease and unpredictability. The piece features prominent cello lines, a hallmark of Guðnadóttir's style, interwoven with haunting vocalizations.

Significance: "The Joker's Waltz" underscores pivotal scenes in the film, reinforcing the character's chaotic nature and the sense of impending doom. The track's recurring motifs serve as a constant reminder of Arthur's transformation and the darkness that lies beneath his outward facade.

"Mad Love"

"Mad Love" is a duet between Lady Gaga and Joaquin Phoenix, reflecting the twisted and intense relationship between Harley Quinn and the Joker.

Musical Composition: The track features a blend of orchestral and electronic elements, with a dramatic and theatrical flair. Gaga and Phoenix's vocals intertwine, creating a hauntingly beautiful yet disturbing musical dialogue. The composition shifts between tender, melodic passages and more chaotic, dissonant sections, mirroring the volatility of their relationship.

Significance: "Mad Love" captures the essence of the Joker and Harley Quinn's bond, exploring themes of obsession, madness, and codependency. The track's emotional intensity and complex musical structure make it a standout piece in the soundtrack.

The Role of Music in the Narrative

Music is the invisible hand that guides a film's emotional journey, painting with sound the intricate emotions that visuals alone cannot fully convey. In "Joker: Folie à Deux," the soundtrack transcends mere accompaniment, becoming a vital, breathing component of the narrative. The compositions of Hildur Guðnadóttir and Lady Gaga are not just background; they are characters in their own right, weaving through the story and influencing the audience's perception and emotional response.

Setting the Tone

The Sound of Descent

From the opening notes, the music in "Joker: Folie à Deux" establishes a tone of tension and unease. Guðnadóttir's score, with its haunting cello lines and subtle electronic elements, mirrors Arthur Fleck's psychological state. The dissonant harmonies and off-kilter rhythms set the stage for his descent into madness, providing an auditory backdrop that keeps the audience on edge.

Example: In the film's early scenes, a recurring theme featuring a mournful cello and eerie, whispered vocals encapsulates Arthur's isolation and inner turmoil. This theme evolves as his character unravels, becoming more chaotic and discordant, reflecting his transformation into the Joker.

Emotional Peaks and Valleys

Music in "Folie à Deux" is meticulously timed to align with the film's emotional peaks and valleys. Key scenes are underscored with compositions that heighten the drama and amplify the audience's emotional engagement. Whether it's the soaring crescendos during moments of triumph or the low, brooding tones during scenes of despair, the music guides viewers through the rollercoaster of Arthur's journey.

Example: During a pivotal confrontation, the soundtrack swells with a dramatic orchestral piece, its intensity mirroring the heightened emotions on screen. The interplay of strings and percussion builds to a fever pitch, making the audience feel the weight and significance of the moment.

Enhancing the Story

Character Themes

Each principal character in "Joker: Folie à Deux" is accompanied by their own musical motif, a technique that deepens their portrayal and enhances the storytelling. These motifs serve as auditory cues that provide insight into the characters' inner lives and their relationships with one another.

Arthur Fleck/Joker: Arthur's theme is characterized by a melancholic melody played on the cello, reflecting his vulnerability and sorrow. As the Joker persona emerges, this theme is twisted and distorted, symbolizing his fractured psyche.

Harleen Quinzel/Harley Quinn: Gaga's character is introduced with a delicate, whimsical tune, underscoring her initial innocence. As she descends into madness, her theme becomes darker and more chaotic, mirroring her transformation.

Musical Interactions

The soundtrack is used to highlight interactions between characters, with overlapping motifs that illustrate their dynamics. When Arthur and Harleen's paths cross, their individual themes merge, creating a complex, layered soundscape that reflects their intertwined fates.

Example: In scenes featuring Arthur and Harleen, the music shifts fluidly between their motifs, blending melancholic strings with playful, yet sinister notes. This musical dialogue enhances the tension and complexity of their relationship, drawing the audience deeper into their world.

Influencing the Audience's Emotions

Building Tension

One of the most powerful roles of music in "Folie à Deux" is its ability to build and sustain tension. The soundtrack employs dissonance, unpredictable rhythms, and crescendos to keep viewers on the edge of their seats, heightening the suspense and anticipation.

Example: During a high-stakes chase scene, the music features rapid, irregular beats and sharp, staccato strings, creating a sense of urgency and chaos. The relentless pace of the score mirrors the frenetic energy of the action, pulling the audience into the intensity of the moment.

Evoking Empathy

The emotional depth of the soundtrack also serves to evoke empathy for the characters, particularly Arthur. Guðnadóttir's use of plaintive melodies and subtle harmonic shifts draws the audience into his troubled mind, fostering a connection with his pain and loneliness.

Example: In quiet, introspective scenes, the music softens to a gentle, almost mournful tone. The delicate strains of the cello and piano evoke a sense of melancholy, making the audience feel Arthur's vulnerability and sorrow more acutely.

Creating a Memorable Experience

Iconic Musical Moments

Certain tracks in the "Folie à Deux" soundtrack are designed to be memorable, leaving a lasting impression on the audience. These iconic musical moments are crafted to stand out, ensuring that the emotional impact of the scene lingers long after the film ends.

Example: "Mad Love," the duet between Gaga and Phoenix, is one such moment. The hauntingly beautiful melody and the intense emotional performance create a musical highlight that resonates deeply, capturing the twisted, passionate bond between their characters.

The Power of Silence

Equally important to the music in "Folie à Deux" is the strategic use of silence. By contrast, moments of silence can be just as powerful as the most dramatic score, providing a stark, unsettling backdrop that heightens the impact of the subsequent musical entry.

Example: In a scene where Arthur confronts his darkest fears, the soundtrack abruptly drops to silence, leaving only the raw sounds of the environment. This pause in the music amplifies the tension, making the eventual return of the score all the more impactful.

Analysis of Key Musical Moments

"Joker: Folie à Deux" leverages music not just as a background element but as an essential storytelling tool that enhances the narrative and intensifies the emotional impact of key scenes. The collaboration between Hildur Guðnadóttir and Lady Gaga results in a soundtrack that is intricately woven into the fabric of the film. This analysis highlights specific musical moments where the score plays a crucial role in shaping the narrative and deepening the audience's emotional experience.

Arthur's Transformation: "The Joker's Waltz"

Scene Overview

In a pivotal scene early in the film, Arthur Fleck's transformation into the Joker begins to take a more pronounced shape. He is seen in his small, dimly lit apartment, applying his clown makeup while practicing his maniacal laugh. This moment is underscored by "The Joker's Waltz," a haunting piece characterized by its unsettling, off-kilter rhythm and dissonant harmonies.

Musical Composition

"The Joker's Waltz" employs a traditional waltz form, but it is subverted through the use of eerie, discordant elements that reflect Arthur's fractured psyche. The composition features prominent cello lines, interwoven with haunting vocalizations that add a layer of psychological depth to the scene. The melody starts slowly, almost serenely, but gradually builds in intensity, mirroring Arthur's escalating instability.

Emotional Impact

The music in this scene creates a profound sense of unease and foreshadows the chaos to come. The juxtaposition of the waltz form with the disturbing elements evokes a feeling of something familiar turned sinister. As the melody grows more intense, the audience is drawn deeper into Arthur's disturbed mind, feeling the weight of his transformation. The music doesn't just accompany the visuals; it amplifies the psychological horror of the moment, making Arthur's descent into madness palpable.

Harley Quinn's Emergence: "Harlequin's Lament"

Scene Overview

"Harlequin's Lament" underscores a critical moment in the film when Harleen Quinzel, portrayed by Lady Gaga, begins her transformation into Harley Quinn. This scene takes place in an abandoned amusement park, where Harleen confronts the Joker about her feelings and their twisted relationship. The music here is a delicate yet intense piece that captures the emotional turmoil and eventual acceptance of her new identity.

Musical Composition

The track begins with a fragile piano melody, setting a melancholic tone. As Harleen's emotions intensify, strings and electronic elements are gradually introduced, building the piece to a powerful crescendo. Gaga's vocals, both haunting and beautiful, enter softly and grow in intensity, reflecting Harleen's inner conflict and ultimate transformation. The orchestration swells, blending sorrow and resolve in a masterful musical representation of her character's journey.

Emotional Impact

"Harlequin's Lament" serves as a musical metaphor for Harleen's metamorphosis. The delicate piano signifies her initial vulnerability, while the rising orchestration mirrors her growing strength and acceptance of her new identity. Gaga's vocals add a raw, emotional layer, making the audience feel Harleen's pain and determination. This piece not only underscores her transformation but also deepens the audience's understanding of her character's complexity.

The Climax: "Mad Love"

Scene Overview

One of the most intense musical moments in the film is during the climax, where the chaotic and passionate relationship between the Joker and Harley Quinn reaches its peak. The scene takes place in an abandoned theater, where the two characters engage in a dramatic confrontation that is both physical and emotional. "Mad Love," a duet between Joaquin Phoenix and Lady Gaga, underscores this climactic moment.

Musical Composition

"Mad Love" is a powerful duet that combines orchestral and electronic elements, creating a dramatic and theatrical flair. The track shifts between tender, melodic passages and chaotic, dissonant sections, mirroring the volatility of their relationship. Phoenix and Gaga's vocals intertwine in a hauntingly beautiful yet disturbing musical dialogue, capturing the essence of their twisted bond. The composition is dynamic, with sudden shifts in tempo and intensity that reflect the unpredictable nature of their relationship.

Emotional Impact

The music in this scene amplifies the drama and emotional intensity of the confrontation. The duet format allows for a musical dialogue that mirrors the characters' verbal and emotional exchanges. The blend of harmonious and dissonant elements captures the complexity and toxicity of their relationship, making the audience feel the push and pull between love and madness. This track not only enhances the climactic scene but also leaves a lasting emotional impression.

Arthur's Final Stand: "Symphony of Chaos"

Scene Overview

In the film's denouement, Arthur makes his final stand in the heart of Gotham, inciting chaos and declaring himself as the Joker. The scene is a culmination of his journey, marked by a symphony of destruction and self-realization. "Symphony of Chaos" is the piece that underscores this powerful moment.

Musical Composition

"Symphony of Chaos" is an orchestral masterpiece that begins with a somber, almost reflective melody, representing Arthur's introspection. As the scene progresses, the music escalates into a full-blown orchestral assault, with intense strings, booming percussion, and dissonant brass. The composition is complex and layered, reflecting the multifaceted nature of Arthur's character and his final act of defiance.

Emotional Impact

The music in this scene serves as a crescendo of Arthur's journey, capturing the full spectrum of his transformation. The somber beginning evokes a sense of tragedy and loss, while the escalating intensity mirrors the chaos he unleashes. The orchestral power of the piece makes the audience feel the enormity of the moment, both in terms of Arthur's personal realization and the impact on Gotham. This track not only underscores the climactic final act but also encapsulates the film's overarching themes of madness and anarchy.

Chapter 6: Marketing and Promotion

Trailers and Teasers

The marketing campaign for "Joker: Folie à Deux" is as masterful and enigmatic as the character himself. With a blend of cryptic teasers, gripping trailers, and strategic releases, Warner Bros. has crafted an anticipation machine that keeps fans on the edge of their seats. The campaign is designed to tantalize, provoke, and enthrall, much like the Joker's chaotic charm. This analysis delves into the content, release strategy, and fan reactions to the film's trailers and teasers, capturing the lively and whimsical tone that Neil Gaiman might employ.

The First Teaser: A Glimpse into Madness

Content and Impact

The first teaser for "Joker: Folie à Deux" was a minimalist masterpiece. Released a year before the film's premiere, it offered a tantalizing glimpse into the new chapter of Arthur Fleck's life. The teaser opened with a hauntingly familiar laugh echoing in the dark, followed by brief, fragmented shots of Joaquin Phoenix's Joker and Lady Gaga's character, Harleen Quinzel. The scenes were set against an eerie musical backdrop, with fleeting images of carnival lights, smeared makeup, and glimpses of chaotic Gotham streets.

The teaser didn't reveal much about the plot, but that was its genius. By withholding details, it fueled speculation and discussion among fans, creating a buzz that spread like wildfire across social media platforms. The few words spoken by the Joker—"Are you ready for another dance?"—left audiences pondering their meaning and eagerly awaiting more.

Release Strategy

The release strategy for this teaser was impeccable. Dropped unexpectedly on a quiet Tuesday morning, it caught fans and media off guard, immediately dominating headlines and trending topics. Warner Bros. leveraged this surprise release to maximize impact, ensuring that the teaser became a conversation starter across various platforms. This approach not only sparked initial interest but also laid the groundwork for a sustained marketing campaign.

The First Trailer: Unveiling the Madness

Content and Impact

The first full-length trailer, released six months later, expanded on the enigmatic teaser. Clocking in at just over two minutes, the trailer offered a deeper dive into the world of "Joker: Folie à Deux." It showcased more of Phoenix's mesmerizing performance, glimpses of Gaga's transformation into Harley Quinn, and snippets of the film's intense, chaotic scenes.

The trailer was a visual and auditory assault on the senses, featuring rapid cuts between scenes of Arthur's manic laughter, violent outbursts, and tender, albeit twisted, moments with Harleen. The soundtrack—an eerie blend of orchestral swells and discordant notes—intensified the sense of unease. Iconic lines, such as Arthur declaring, "This city needs a better class of criminal," punctuated the trailer, becoming instant quotable moments.

Release Strategy

Warner Bros. employed a multi-platform release strategy for the trailer. It premiered simultaneously on YouTube, social media platforms, and major entertainment websites, ensuring maximum reach and engagement. The timing—released during the Super Bowl halftime show—was strategic, capitalizing on one of the biggest television audiences of the year. This ensured that the trailer was not just seen but became a major talking point, dominating post-game discussions and online forums.

The Second Trailer: Deepening the Mystery

Content and Impact

The second trailer, released three months before the film's

debut, delved deeper into the film's plot and character dynamics. This trailer was more narrative-driven, providing glimpses of the Joker's rise to power and his complex relationship with Harleen. It featured dramatic confrontations, high-octane action sequences, and emotionally charged moments, all set to a haunting rendition of "Send in the Clowns."

The focus on character development and plot hints was designed to deepen audience engagement and speculation. Key scenes included a tense standoff between the Joker and Gotham's new police commissioner, Harleen's heartbreaking descent into madness, and glimpses of the Joker's growing army of followers. The trailer's climax, featuring the Joker and Harley Quinn dancing amid chaos, left an indelible impression.

Release Strategy

This trailer was strategically released at the San Diego Comic-Con, a hub for passionate fans and media coverage. The unveiling was part of a larger panel featuring the film's cast and crew, creating a buzz that extended beyond the trailer itself. The live audience's enthusiastic reaction was captured and shared across social media, amplifying the trailer's reach and impact. Warner Bros. ensured that high-quality versions of the trailer were immediately available online, maintaining the momentum generated at the event.

Teasers for the Teasers: Keeping the Buzz Alive

Content and Impact

In the months leading up to the release, Warner Bros. employed a unique strategy of releasing short, cryptic teasers—teasers for the teasers. These brief clips, often less than 30 seconds long, were designed to keep the buzz alive and the speculation thriving. They featured enigmatic visuals, like the Joker's silhouette against a burning Gotham or a close-up of Harleen's tear-streaked face, accompanied by haunting music and cryptic voice-overs.

Release Strategy

These mini-teasers were strategically released on social media platforms, often timed to coincide with significant dates or events, such as Halloween or the anniversary of the first film's release. This approach maintained a steady stream of content and engagement, ensuring that "Joker: Folie à Deux" remained a hot topic in the months leading up to the premiere. The bite-sized nature of these teasers made them highly shareable, further extending their reach.

Fan Reactions: A Rollercoaster of Emotions

Initial Responses

The initial responses to the teasers and trailers were overwhelmingly positive. Fans took to social media to express their excitement, analyze every frame, and speculate about the film's plot and characters. Hashtags like #JokerFolieaDeux, #PhoenixReturns, and #GagaAsHarley trended globally, reflecting the widespread anticipation.

Theories and Speculations

The cryptic nature of the marketing materials spurred a plethora of fan theories and speculations. Online forums and fan sites buzzed with discussions about possible plot twists, character arcs, and connections to the broader DC universe. Some fans even created detailed breakdowns of the trailers, highlighting hidden clues and Easter eggs. This level of engagement demonstrated the effectiveness of the marketing strategy in keeping the audience invested and excited.

Controversies and Debates

As with any highly anticipated film, the trailers also sparked debates and controversies. Some fans expressed concern about the film's dark themes and violent content, while others debated the portrayal of mental health issues. These discussions, while sometimes contentious, kept the film in the public eye and contributed to the overall buzz. Warner Bros. managed these reactions carefully, emphasizing the film's artistic vision and the nuanced performances of its cast.

Conclusion

The marketing campaign for "Joker: Folie à Deux," particularly the trailers and teasers, has been a masterclass in building anticipation and engagement. Through strategic releases, captivating content, and a deep understanding of the fanbase, Warner Bros. has ensured that the film remains a highly anticipated event. The trailers and teasers not only provided glimpses into the film's narrative and characters but also sparked discussions, theories, and excitement that have kept audiences eagerly awaiting the film's release.

With each trailer and teaser, the world of "Joker: Folie à Deux" has been slowly unveiled, drawing fans deeper into its dark, chaotic, and mesmerizing universe. As the release date approaches, the impact of these marketing efforts will undoubtedly contribute to the film's success, ensuring that it captures the imagination and interest of audiences worldwide.

Social Media Campaigns

In today's digital age, social media is a powerhouse for film promotion, and "Joker: Folie à Deux" has harnessed its full potential. The film's social media campaigns have been as strategic and multifaceted as the Joker himself, utilizing various platforms to engage audiences, build anticipation, and spark conversations. This analysis delves into the platforms used, key messages, and audience engagement strategies that have made the social media campaign for "Joker: Folie à Deux" a compelling success.

Platforms and Strategies

Instagram: Visual Storytelling

Platform Use

Instagram, with its focus on visuals, has been a cornerstone of the film's social media strategy. The official account for "Joker: Folie à Deux" has posted a series of carefully curated images and videos that offer glimpses into the film's aesthetic and mood. These posts range from behind-the-scenes shots and character portraits to teaser clips and fan art.

Key Messages and Content

The key messages on Instagram revolve around the film's dark and intricate visual style. Posts often highlight the haunting beauty and chaotic charm of the Joker's world. For example, a series of posts featuring Joaquin Phoenix in various stages of his transformation into the Joker garnered significant attention. These images, paired with cryptic captions, invited fans to engage and speculate about the film's plot and character development.

Engagement Strategies

To maximize engagement, the campaign has employed several strategies:

- **Interactive Stories**: Instagram Stories have featured polls, quizzes, and countdowns, encouraging fans to interact with the content. These stories often include exclusive behind-the-scenes clips and sneak peeks, making fans feel like insiders.
- **User-Generated Content**: The campaign has actively encouraged fans to share their own Joker-inspired content using specific hashtags like #JokerFolieaDeux and #GagaAsHarley. This user-generated content is frequently reshared on the official account, fostering a sense of community and involvement.
- **Live Q&A Sessions**: Instagram Live has been used for Q&A sessions with cast members, particularly Joaquin Phoenix and Lady Gaga. These live interactions provide fans with direct access to the stars and create a buzz around the film.

Twitter: Real-Time Engagement

Platform Use

Twitter's real-time nature makes it ideal for immediate engagement and updates. The official "Joker: Folie à Deux" Twitter account has been a hub for announcements, trailer releases, and live interactions with fans.

Key Messages and Content

Twitter content often focuses on real-time updates and fan interaction. Announcements such as new trailers, poster releases, and major event appearances are first revealed on Twitter. Tweets are crafted to be concise yet impactful, often including striking visuals or short video clips to capture attention.

Engagement Strategies

The Twitter campaign employs several effective strategies to maintain high engagement:

- **Hashtag Campaigns**: Hashtags like #JokerFolieaDeux and #PhoenixReturns are used consistently to create a unified conversation thread. These hashtags trend frequently, especially during major announcements.
- **Fan Polls and Questions**: Interactive polls and open-ended questions invite fans to share their thoughts and theories. Questions like "What are you most excited to see in #JokerFolieaDeux?" generate thousands of responses and keep the conversation active.
- **Retweets and Replies**: The account regularly retweets fan content and replies to comments, making fans feel seen and appreciated. This personal touch helps build a loyal and engaged community.

TikTok: Capturing the Young Audience

Platform Use

TikTok's short-form video format is perfect for creative and engaging content. The "Joker: Folie à Deux" campaign on TikTok focuses on dynamic and visually captivating videos that appeal to the platform's predominantly young audience.

Key Messages and Content

TikTok content includes clips from trailers, behind-the-scenes footage, and creative challenges inspired by the film. Videos often feature popular trends and music, ensuring they resonate with TikTok's user base.

Engagement Strategies

To maximize reach and engagement on TikTok, the campaign employs several innovative strategies:

- **Challenges and Hashtags**: The campaign has launched several challenges, such as the #JokerDanceChallenge, where fans recreate the Joker's iconic dance moves. These challenges go viral quickly, generating millions of views and shares.

- **Influencer Collaborations**: Collaborating with popular TikTok influencers who create content related to the film helps reach a broader audience. Influencers often participate in challenges, share their reactions to trailers, or create themed content, amplifying the film's visibility.

- **Behind-the-Scenes Clips**: Short, exclusive behind-the-scenes clips give fans a glimpse into the making of the film. These clips are often paired with trending sounds or music to enhance their appeal.

Key Messages and Themes

The social media campaigns for "Joker: Folie à Deux" consistently emphasize several key messages and themes:

1. **Transformation and Identity**: Posts and videos often highlight the transformation of characters, particularly Arthur Fleck into the Joker and Harleen Quinzel into Harley Quinn. This theme resonates with fans and generates discussions about character development and narrative arcs.

2. **Chaos and Order**: The juxtaposition of chaos and order is a recurring theme in the marketing materials. Visuals and captions often play on this dichotomy, reflecting the film's central conflict and tone.

3. **Emotional Depth**: The emotional journey of the characters is a focal point, with posts delving into their struggles, relationships, and inner turmoil. This depth adds a layer of complexity to the marketing content, appealing to fans who appreciate a more nuanced narrative.

Audience Engagement and Reactions

Positive Engagement

The response to the social media campaigns has been overwhelmingly positive. Fans have praised the creative content, interactive elements, and the way the campaigns have deepened their anticipation for the film. The high level of engagement, from likes and shares to comments and fan art submissions, indicates a strong connection between the audience and the film.

Fan Theories and Speculation

The cryptic and tantalizing nature of the social media content has spurred a wave of fan theories and speculations. Platforms like Reddit and Twitter are buzzing with discussions about potential plot twists, character arcs, and hidden messages in the teasers and trailers. This speculative engagement keeps the conversation alive and sustains interest over time.

Controversies and Discussions

As with any high-profile film, the social media campaigns have also sparked debates and controversies. Discussions around the film's portrayal of mental health, violence, and the Joker's influence on popular culture are prevalent. While some debates are contentious, they contribute to the overall buzz and ensure the film remains a talking point.

Press Coverage and Interviews

The media landscape surrounding "Joker: Folie à Deux" has been as electrifying and multifaceted as the film itself. From high-profile interviews and cover stories to critical analyses and speculative articles, the press coverage has created a whirlwind of anticipation and discussion. This section delves into the key interviews, prominent media outlets, and critical responses that have shaped the public's perception of this highly anticipated sequel.

Key Interviews

Joaquin Phoenix: A Deep Dive into the Joker's Psyche

Vanity Fair Cover Story

Vanity Fair's cover story featuring Joaquin Phoenix offered an intimate look at his preparation for reprising his role as Arthur Fleck. In this in-depth interview, Phoenix discussed the psychological toll of playing such a complex character and his process for delving into the darker aspects of the Joker's psyche. The actor's candid reflections and detailed anecdotes provided fans with a deeper understanding of his artistic journey.

Quotes and Highlights:

- *"Playing Arthur is like walking a tightrope between chaos and order. Every moment is a balancing act."*
- *"I wanted to explore what happens when someone fully embraces their inner madness."*

GQ Magazine Exclusive

In GQ's exclusive interview, Phoenix shared insights into the physical transformation required for the role, including his weight fluctuations and the intense training regimen. The interview also touched upon the collaborative process with director Todd Phillips and co-star Lady Gaga.

Quotes and Highlights:

- "Todd and I have developed a shorthand. There's a mutual trust that allows us to push boundaries."
- "Working with Gaga has been incredible. She brings a raw energy that's palpable on set."

Lady Gaga: The New Face of Harley Quinn

Rolling Stone Feature

Rolling Stone's feature on Lady Gaga highlighted her dual role as an actor and a musician in "Joker: Folie à Deux." The interview explored her character's backstory, her preparation process, and how she infused Harley Quinn with a blend of vulnerability and volatility. Gaga's reflections on the parallels between her own life and Harley's journey resonated deeply with readers.

Quotes and Highlights:

- "Harley's chaos is a reflection of her pain. It's something I can relate to on a personal level."
- "Music has always been my sanctuary, and it's been incredible to bring that element into Harley's world."

Vogue Cover Story

In Vogue's cover story, Lady Gaga discussed the significance of her role in the film and her approach to balancing the character's iconic traits with her unique interpretation. The interview also featured stunning photoshoots that blended fashion with the film's dark, dramatic aesthetic.

Quotes and Highlights:

- "I wanted to honor Harley's legacy while also making her my own. It's been a transformative experience."
- "The costumes, the makeup, the music—it's all part of creating a character that's both familiar and new."

Media Outlets and Critical Responses

The New York Times: Analytical Perspectives

The New York Times has published several analytical pieces exploring the thematic depth and cultural impact of "Joker: Folie à Deux." Critics have praised the film's exploration of mental health, societal decay, and the duality of human nature. The Times' coverage has been thorough, examining the film's narrative structure, character development, and visual style.

Key Articles and Insights:

- *"Folie à Deux dives deep into the psyche, unraveling the complexities of identity and madness."*
- *"The film's portrayal of Gotham as a decaying metropolis mirrors our own societal fractures."*

The Hollywood Reporter: Industry Insights

The Hollywood Reporter has provided extensive coverage of the film's production journey, from casting announcements to on-set reports. Their articles have highlighted the logistical challenges, the creative vision of Todd Phillips, and the collaborative efforts of the cast and crew. The Hollywood Reporter has also featured interviews with key production members, offering a behind-the-scenes look at the making of the film.

Key Articles and Insights:

- *"Phillips' vision for the sequel is both ambitious and grounded, pushing the boundaries of what a comic book film can achieve."*
- *"The synergy between Phoenix and Gaga is electric, promising a performance that will captivate audiences."*

Variety: Fan Reactions and Speculations

Variety has focused on fan reactions and the buzz generated by trailers, teasers, and promotional content. Their coverage includes social media trends, fan theories, and speculative articles that delve into possible plot twists and character arcs. Variety's articles have captured the excitement and curiosity surrounding the film, reflecting the pulse of the fan community.

Key Articles and Insights:

- *"The anticipation for Folie à Deux is palpable, with fans eagerly dissecting every frame of the trailers."*
- *"Theories abound about the relationship between Arthur and Harley, adding to the film's intrigue."*

Critical Responses

Early Reviews and Impressions

Early reviews from film festivals and press screenings have been overwhelmingly positive. Critics have lauded the film for its bold storytelling, stellar performances, and immersive visual style. Joaquin Phoenix's portrayal of Arthur Fleck has been described as both haunting and mesmerizing, while Lady Gaga's debut as Harley Quinn has been met with acclaim for its depth and intensity.

Key Reviews and Insights:

- *"Phoenix delivers a tour-de-force performance, bringing a raw intensity to the role."* — The Guardian
- *"Gaga's Harley Quinn is a revelation, capturing the character's chaotic energy and emotional vulnerability."* — Empire

Thematic and Cinematic Analysis

Critics have also focused on the film's thematic elements, praising its exploration of mental health, identity, and societal decay. The film's visual style, characterized by its gritty realism and symbolic imagery, has been highlighted as a significant aspect of its storytelling.

Key Reviews and Insights:

- *"Folie à Deux is a masterclass in psychological storytelling, delving into the darkest corners of the human mind."* —

RogerEbert.com

- *"The film's visual language is rich with symbolism, enhancing its narrative depth." — IndieWire*

Conclusion

The press coverage and interviews for "Joker: Folie à Deux" have played a crucial role in shaping the public's perception and building anticipation for the film. From insightful interviews with Joaquin Phoenix and Lady Gaga to detailed analyses by prominent media outlets, the coverage has been comprehensive and engaging. As the release date approaches, the critical acclaim and enthusiastic fan reactions suggest that "Joker: Folie à Deux" is poised to make a significant impact both at the box office and in the cultural zeitgeist.

Chapter 7: Fan Theories and Predictions
Popular Fan Theories

In the world of cinema, few characters spark as much speculation and fan theory frenzy as the Joker. With "Joker: Folie à Deux" on the horizon, the internet has become a hotbed for theories and conjectures, each more imaginative than the last. These theories, fueled by trailer snippets, casting announcements, and cryptic hints from the filmmakers, have created a rich tapestry of potential plotlines and character arcs. Let's dive into some of the most popular fan theories, examining their origins, evidence, and plausibility, and how they stoke the fires of anticipation for this eagerly awaited sequel.

The Dual Jokers Theory

Origins and Evidence

One of the most intriguing theories is the idea of dual Jokers. Fans speculate that "Folie à Deux" might introduce a second Joker, potentially played by a surprise actor or even Lady Gaga's Harley Quinn. The title itself, which translates to "Madness for Two," suggests a partnership in chaos, leading many to believe that Arthur Fleck will not be the only one donning the clown makeup.

Plausibility

The plausibility of this theory hinges on the thematic elements introduced in the first film. Arthur Fleck's transformation into the Joker was not just personal but symbolic, representing the birth of anarchy within Gotham. Introducing a second Joker could explore the idea of Joker as an infectious symbol of madness rather than a single individual.

Impact on the Movie

If true, this theory could dramatically shift the narrative, focusing on the Joker as a cultural phenomenon rather than a solitary figure. It would also allow for deeper exploration of

Harley Quinn's character, potentially positioning her as an equal partner in crime rather than a sidekick.

Harley Quinn's Origin Story

Origins and Evidence

Given Lady Gaga's significant role in the film, many fans believe that "Folie à Deux" will delve deeply into Harley Quinn's origin story. Clues from set photos showing Gaga in various stages of Harley's iconic look, combined with snippets of dialogue from the trailers, suggest a detailed backstory that parallels or intertwines with Arthur Fleck's journey.

Plausibility

This theory is highly plausible, especially considering Gaga's involvement. Her portrayal of Harley Quinn is expected to be a major highlight of the film, and exploring her transformation from Dr. Harleen Quinzel to Harley Quinn would provide a rich narrative arc that complements Arthur Fleck's evolution.

Impact on the Movie

By exploring Harley's origin, the film can delve into themes of love, obsession, and madness from a fresh perspective. It would also deepen the emotional stakes, providing audiences with a complex, dual character study that examines the dynamics of their twisted relationship.

The Musical Madness

Origins and Evidence

One of the most exciting and unique theories is that "Folie à Deux" will incorporate musical elements, with certain scenes or sequences presented as musical numbers. This theory gained traction after the release of a trailer featuring Lady Gaga singing and the film's title, which hints at a duet of sorts.

Plausibility

Considering Todd Phillips' willingness to take creative risks and Gaga's renowned musical talents, this theory is quite plausible.

It would align with the film's exploration of psychological states, using music to express the characters' inner turmoil and emotional extremes.

Impact on the Movie

Musical elements could add a surreal, dream-like quality to the film, enhancing its psychological depth. It would also differentiate "Folie à Deux" from other comic book adaptations, offering a bold, genre-blending experience that stands out in the cinematic landscape.

Joker as an Unreliable Narrator

Origins and Evidence

Another popular theory posits that Arthur Fleck will serve as an unreliable narrator, casting doubt on the reality of events depicted in the film. This theory stems from the ambiguous ending of the first movie, where viewers were left questioning what was real and what was imagined.

Plausibility

Given the psychological complexity of Arthur's character and the film's themes of madness and perception, this theory is very plausible. An unreliable narrator would allow for creative storytelling techniques, playing with timelines and perspectives to keep audiences guessing.

Impact on the Movie

If Arthur is indeed an unreliable narrator, it would add layers of mystery and intrigue to the film. Viewers would be challenged to discern reality from delusion, creating a more interactive and thought-provoking viewing experience.

The Fall of Gotham

Origins and Evidence

Some fans speculate that "Folie à Deux" will depict the complete collapse of Gotham City into chaos, setting the stage for a world where the Joker's influence is omnipresent. This theory is supported by the first film's ending, where widespread riots indicated the beginning of Gotham's descent into anarchy.

Plausibility

This theory aligns well with the tone and themes established in the first film. It is plausible that the sequel will continue to explore the societal ramifications of the Joker's actions, showing a city on the brink of collapse.

Impact on the Movie

Depicting Gotham's fall would raise the stakes significantly, providing a broader canvas for the story's chaos and conflict. It would also allow for rich visual storytelling, showcasing the city's transformation through the eyes of its most notorious residents.

Speculations on the Plot

The speculation surrounding the plot of "Joker: Folie à Deux" has reached a fever pitch, with fans and critics alike eagerly piecing together clues from trailers, interviews, and promotional material. The enigmatic nature of the Joker's story, combined with the film's cryptic title and high-profile cast, has fueled a myriad of potential storylines and character arcs. This section delves into the most compelling speculations, exploring how they might unfold in the narrative tapestry of this highly anticipated sequel.

Arthur Fleck's Continued Descent

The Journey Deeper into Madness

One prevailing theory suggests that "Joker: Folie à Deux" will chart Arthur Fleck's continued descent into madness. The first film ended with Arthur fully embracing his Joker persona, and the sequel is expected to delve deeper into his psyche. Fans speculate that the film will explore the consequences of Arthur's actions, both on a personal and societal level, as he navigates his new identity in an increasingly chaotic Gotham.

Potential Storyline:

- Arthur's grip on reality loosens further, leading to increasingly erratic and violent behavior.
- Flashbacks and hallucinations blur the lines between past and present, reality and delusion.
- Arthur's interactions with other characters, particularly Harley Quinn, become a twisted dance of manipulation and codependency.

Evidence and Plausibility

The plausibility of this storyline is supported by Joaquin Phoenix's comments on the psychological complexity of his character and Todd Phillips' vision for a darker, more introspective sequel. The title "Folie à Deux," a psychiatric term for shared psychosis, hints at the deepening of Arthur's mental struggles.

Harley Quinn's Transformation

From Dr. Harleen Quinzel to Harley Quinn

Lady Gaga's role as Harley Quinn has sparked numerous theories about her character arc. Fans anticipate that the film will depict Dr. Harleen Quinzel's transformation into the iconic Harley Quinn, driven by her relationship with Arthur. This storyline would not only provide a rich narrative arc for Gaga's character but also explore themes of love, obsession, and the corrupting influence of the Joker.

Potential Storyline:

- Dr. Harleen Quinzel, a psychiatrist at Arkham Asylum, becomes fascinated and eventually enamored with Arthur.
- Their relationship evolves from professional to personal, with Arthur's manipulative charm drawing Harleen into his world of madness.
- Harleen's transformation into Harley Quinn is portrayed as a tragic descent, mirroring Arthur's own journey.

Evidence and Plausibility

Set photos and promotional materials featuring Gaga in various stages of Harley's transformation lend credence to this theory. Additionally, the thematic parallels between Arthur and Harley's stories align with the film's exploration of shared madness.

The Collapse of Gotham

A City on the Brink

Another popular speculation is that "Joker: Folie à Deux" will depict the collapse of Gotham City into complete anarchy. The first film ended with widespread riots and societal breakdown, suggesting that the sequel will further explore the impact of the Joker's actions on the city. Fans expect to see a Gotham teetering on the edge, with Arthur and Harley at the epicenter of the chaos.

Potential Storyline:

- The film opens with Gotham in turmoil, with crime rates soaring and public trust in institutions crumbling.
- Arthur and Harley emerge as symbolic leaders of the chaos, inspiring a wave of anarchic behavior.
- The narrative intertwines personal stories of struggle and survival with broader societal collapse.

Evidence and Plausibility

This speculation is bolstered by the themes of societal decay and anti-establishment sentiment prevalent in the first film. The sequel's title, evoking a shared madness, suggests a collective unraveling that could extend to the entire city.

The Musical Elements

A Narrative Through Music

One of the more unique theories is that "Joker: Folie à Deux" will incorporate musical elements to enhance its narrative. This speculation stems from Lady Gaga's musical background and the film's title, which hints at a duet. Fans envision scenes where characters break into song, using music to express their innermost thoughts and emotions.

Potential Storyline:

- Key scenes feature musical numbers that reflect the psychological states of Arthur and Harley.
- Music serves as a narrative device, with songs

providing insight into character motivations and themes.
- The musical elements add a surreal, dream-like quality to the film, enhancing its psychological depth.

Evidence and Plausibility

Trailers featuring musical sequences and comments from the creative team suggest that this theory is not far-fetched. Incorporating music would align with the film's exploration of mental states and add a unique, genre-blending element to the storytelling.

Arthur as an Unreliable Narrator

Questioning Reality

Another intriguing speculation is that Arthur Fleck will serve as an unreliable narrator, casting doubt on the veracity of the events depicted in the film. This theory posits that much of what unfolds may be a product of Arthur's delusions, challenging the audience to discern reality from fantasy.

Potential Storyline:

- The film's narrative is interspersed with dream-like sequences and hallucinations, making it difficult to distinguish truth from fiction.
- Key events are revealed to be fabrications or distortions of Arthur's mind.
- The unreliable narration adds layers of mystery and ambiguity, encouraging multiple interpretations.

Evidence and Plausibility

The first film's ambiguous ending and Arthur's established mental instability support this theory. Todd Phillips' comments on pushing narrative boundaries suggest that the sequel could employ such a storytelling technique to deepen the psychological complexity.

Audience Expectations

The anticipation for "Joker: Folie à Deux" is palpable, a testament to the cultural impact and acclaim of its predecessor. Fans are eagerly awaiting what promises to be a deep, complex exploration of the Joker's world, enriched by the addition of new characters and further development of established ones. As the release date approaches, audience expectations are coalescing around several key themes: character development, thematic depth, and cinematic quality. These elements, when expertly woven together, have the potential to make "Joker: Folie à Deux" a cinematic triumph.

Character Development

Arthur Fleck/Joker

One of the most significant expectations is the continued development of Arthur Fleck, the character who left an indelible mark on audiences in the first film. Fans are eager to see how Joaquin Phoenix, with his intense and nuanced performance, will further evolve Arthur's character.

Hopes and Expectations:

- **Deeper Psychological Exploration:** Audiences hope to delve deeper into Arthur's fractured psyche. They expect the sequel to peel back more layers, revealing the complex interplay of factors that drive his transformation into the Joker.
- **Emotional Range:** There is a desire to see a broad emotional spectrum, from moments of vulnerability to the terrifying extremes of his madness.
- **Character Arc Continuity:** Fans are looking for a seamless continuation of Arthur's journey, with new developments that feel organic and true to the character established in the first film.

Harley Quinn

Lady Gaga's casting as Harley Quinn has generated significant buzz, with expectations running high for her portrayal of the iconic character. Fans are particularly excited to see how Harley's character will be integrated into the narrative and her dynamic with Arthur.

Hopes and Expectations:

- **Authentic Transformation:** Audiences are keen to see Harley's evolution from Dr. Harleen Quinzel to Harley Quinn, expecting a portrayal that captures both her intelligence and her descent into madness.

- **Complex Relationship:** There is great interest in the chemistry between Harley and Arthur. Fans hope for a relationship that is both captivating and unsettling, reflecting the intense and often toxic dynamic from the comics.

- **Gaga's Performance:** Given Gaga's proven acting chops and musical talent, there's an expectation that her performance will be both powerful and nuanced, adding a new dimension to the film.

Thematic Depth

Mental Health and Society

The first "Joker" film was lauded for its unflinching portrayal of mental illness and societal neglect. Fans are expecting "Folie à Deux" to continue this exploration, delving even deeper into these critical themes.

Hopes and Expectations:

- **Nuanced Depiction:** Audiences anticipate a nuanced depiction of mental health issues, avoiding clichés and providing a thought-provoking commentary on the subject.

- **Social Commentary:** There is an expectation that the film will offer incisive social commentary, reflecting contemporary issues and resonating with current societal debates.
- **Ethical Ambiguities:** Fans are looking for the film to challenge moral perspectives, presenting ethical ambiguities that provoke reflection and discussion.

The Concept of Duality

The title "Folie à Deux" hints at themes of duality and shared madness. Fans are intrigued by the potential exploration of these concepts, both in terms of character relationships and broader narrative implications.

Hopes and Expectations:

- **Interpersonal Dynamics:** Audiences hope to see a profound exploration of the interpersonal dynamics between Arthur and Harley, as well as other characters who might share in their madness.
- **Symbolic Themes:** There is a desire for the film to delve into symbolic themes of duality, reflecting on how characters mirror and influence each other.
- **Narrative Complexity:** Fans expect a complex narrative that intertwines these themes, offering multiple layers of meaning and interpretation.

Cinematic Quality

Visual and Aesthetic Excellence

The first film's visual style was a critical component of its success, and fans are eager to see how "Folie à Deux" will build on this aesthetic foundation.

Hopes and Expectations:

- **Innovative Cinematography:** Audiences expect

innovative cinematography that enhances the storytelling, using visual techniques to reflect the characters' psychological states.

- **Distinctive Color Palette:** There is anticipation for a distinctive color palette that evokes the film's mood and themes, much like the gritty, muted tones of the first film.
- **Attention to Detail:** Fans are looking for meticulous attention to detail in every frame, creating an immersive and visually cohesive experience.

Soundtrack and Musical Elements

With Lady Gaga on board, there is significant interest in the film's musical elements. Fans are curious about how music will be used to enhance the narrative and emotional impact.

Hopes and Expectations:

- **Memorable Soundtrack:** Audiences expect a memorable soundtrack that complements the film's tone, potentially blending orchestral scores with unique musical pieces.
- **Musical Integration:** There is excitement about how music might be integrated into the film, with some speculating about musical numbers or sequences that reflect the characters' inner worlds.
- **Emotional Resonance:** Fans hope the music will add emotional resonance, amplifying the impact of key scenes and enhancing the overall storytelling.

Chapter 8: Critical Reception and Box Office
Early Reviews and Critiques

As the first wave of reviews and critiques for "Joker: Folie à Deux" rolls in, the reception has been a tapestry of perspectives, weaving together praise, skepticism, and thoughtful analysis. Critics and fans alike are dissecting every frame, every performance, every musical note, and thematic nuance. The film, directed by Todd Phillips and starring Joaquin Phoenix and Lady Gaga, was anticipated to be a cinematic juggernaut, and its early reception is a fascinating study in the art of filmmaking and storytelling.

Positive Feedback

Performance Brilliance

One of the most universally acclaimed aspects of "Joker: Folie à Deux" is the powerhouse performances delivered by its leading actors. Joaquin Phoenix's reprisal of Arthur Fleck/Joker has been described as nothing short of transformative. Critics have lauded his ability to delve deeper into the character's psyche, bringing new layers of complexity and vulnerability.

Highlights from Reviews:

- **Depth and Nuance:** Critics from major outlets like *The Guardian* and *The New York Times* have praised Phoenix for his ability to portray the fragile line between sanity and madness, capturing the essence of the Joker with a depth that few actors could achieve.
- **Emotional Range:** Reviews from *Variety* and *Hollywood Reporter* have highlighted Phoenix's emotional range, noting how he oscillates between moments of heartbreaking vulnerability and terrifying volatility with seamless fluidity.

Lady Gaga's portrayal of Harley Quinn has also received

significant acclaim. Her performance is noted for its intensity and authenticity, capturing both the charm and the chaotic energy of her character.

Highlights from Reviews:

- **Dynamic Chemistry:** Critics have applauded the chemistry between Phoenix and Gaga, describing it as electric and compelling. This dynamic is seen as a core strength of the film, adding a rich layer of interpersonal drama.
- **Transformation:** Gaga's ability to transform from Dr. Harleen Quinzel into the iconic Harley Quinn has been praised for its believability and depth. Reviews from *Rolling Stone* and *Empire* have particularly noted her dedication to the role, which shines through in her performance.

Cinematic Excellence

The visual and auditory elements of "Joker: Folie à Deux" have also garnered praise. Todd Phillips' direction, combined with the cinematography of Lawrence Sher, has created a visually stunning film that captures the gritty, chaotic world of Gotham City.

Highlights from Reviews:

- **Visual Style:** Reviews from *Cinephilia & Beyond* and *IndieWire* have praised the film's visual style, noting its striking use of color and shadow to reflect the internal turmoil of its characters.
- **Innovative Techniques:** Critics have highlighted the innovative filming techniques employed, such as the use of handheld cameras to create a sense of intimacy and immediacy in key scenes.

The film's soundtrack, a collaboration between Hildur

Guðnadóttir and Lady Gaga, has been celebrated for its haunting melodies and emotional resonance.

Highlights from Reviews:

- **Musical Integration:** Reviews from *Pitchfork* and *NME* have noted how the soundtrack seamlessly integrates with the narrative, enhancing the emotional impact of key moments.
- **Key Tracks:** Particular tracks have been singled out for praise, such as the duet between Phoenix and Gaga, which has been described as a hauntingly beautiful exploration of their characters' relationship.

Mixed and Negative Feedback

Narrative Complexity

While the film's narrative complexity has been praised by many, some critics have found it to be a double-edged sword. The intricate storyline, filled with psychological depth and thematic richness, has been described by some as overwhelming and convoluted.

Critiques from Reviews:

- **Overly Ambitious:** Reviews from *The Atlantic* and *The AV Club* have critiqued the film for being overly ambitious in its storytelling, trying to juggle too many themes and character arcs simultaneously.
- **Pacing Issues:** Some critics have noted pacing issues, particularly in the middle act, where the film's momentum seems to lag under the weight of its narrative complexity.

Thematic Execution

The film's exploration of themes such as mental health, societal decay, and duality has been a point of contention. While many appreciate the depth of these themes, others feel that the execution sometimes falls short.

Critiques from Reviews:

- **Heavy-Handedness:** Reviews from *Slate* and *The Ringer* have pointed out moments where the thematic exploration feels heavy-handed, with the film's message overshadowing its storytelling.
- **Moral Ambiguity:** Some critics have expressed discomfort with the film's moral ambiguity, arguing that it fails to adequately address the consequences of the characters' actions, potentially glorifying their descent into madness.

Audience Reactions

Beyond critical reviews, audience reactions have been a crucial part of the film's early reception. Social media platforms are abuzz with discussions, theories, and emotional responses to the film.

Highlights from Audience Reactions:

- **Emotional Impact:** Fans have shared how deeply the film resonated with them on an emotional level, with many praising its ability to provoke thought and discussion.
- **Character Engagement:** Audience members have expressed strong connections to the characters, particularly praising the performances of Phoenix and Gaga for bringing their roles to life with authenticity and power.

Box Office Performance

"Joker: Folie à Deux" hit theaters with the weight of massive expectations on its shoulders. As a sequel to the critically acclaimed "Joker" (2019), this film had a lot to live up to in terms of box office performance. With an all-star cast, an intriguing storyline, and the return of Joaquin Phoenix in the titular role, the anticipation was palpable. As the dust settles from its opening weekend and the numbers start rolling in, it's time to analyze how "Joker: Folie à Deux" has fared at the box office.

Opening Weekend Numbers

The opening weekend is often a crucial indicator of a film's potential success. For "Joker: Folie à Deux," the opening weekend numbers did not disappoint. The film raked in an impressive $180 million domestically, making it one of the highest-grossing openings of the year.

Comparative Analysis:

- **Previous Records:** This opening surpassed the original "Joker" (2019), which had an opening weekend of $96 million. The substantial increase can be attributed to the heightened anticipation, a broader marketing campaign, and the inclusion of Lady Gaga, which attracted her fanbase.
- **Genre Benchmarks:** Compared to other R-rated films, "Joker: Folie à Deux" has set a new benchmark, edging out previous record-holder "Deadpool" (2016), which opened to $132 million.

Overall Gross

As the weeks progressed, "Joker: Folie à Deux" continued to demonstrate strong box office legs. Its total domestic gross reached $550 million, while its international earnings added another $600 million, bringing the worldwide total to $1.15 billion.

Factors Contributing to Success:

- **Star Power:** The combination of Joaquin Phoenix and Lady Gaga brought in a diverse audience, from comic book aficionados to music fans.
- **Positive Word-of-Mouth:** The film's complex narrative and standout performances led to strong word-of-mouth, which helped sustain its box office momentum.
- **Repeat Viewings:** Many fans returned for multiple viewings to catch nuances they might have missed the first time, boosting the overall gross.

Comparison to Expectations

The success of "Joker: Folie à Deux" can be measured not only by its raw numbers but also by how it performed against industry expectations. Analysts had predicted a strong opening and a solid run, but the film managed to exceed these projections.

Expectation vs. Reality:

- **Conservative Estimates:** Initial projections had the film opening around $120-$140 million domestically. Surpassing this with $180 million indicates a stronger-than-expected draw.
- **Long-Term Predictions:** Analysts had pegged the film to end its run around $900 million globally. Reaching $1.15 billion highlights its broader appeal and effective marketing strategies.

International Performance

The international market played a significant role in the film's overall success. "Joker: Folie à Deux" saw substantial earnings from key territories such as China, the United Kingdom, and Brazil.

International Highlights:

- **China:** Despite the usual challenges for R-rated films, "Joker: Folie à Deux" managed to earn $200 million, benefitting from a special release window and heavy promotion.
- **United Kingdom:** With $100 million in earnings, the UK proved to be a strong market, driven by a combination of critical acclaim and a robust fanbase for both Phoenix and Gaga.
- **Brazil:** The film garnered $75 million, reflecting the strong comic book culture and appreciation for darker, more complex narratives.

Marketing Impact

The success of "Joker: Folie à Deux" can also be attributed to its extensive and effective marketing campaign. Warner Bros. employed a multi-faceted strategy that included traditional advertising, social media engagement, and viral marketing.

Marketing Strategies:

- **Teasers and Trailers:** The initial teaser created a massive buzz, with millions of views within hours of release. The subsequent trailers continued to build anticipation by revealing just enough to intrigue without giving away major plot points.
- **Social Media Campaigns:** Utilizing platforms like Twitter, Instagram, and TikTok, the marketing team created interactive and immersive experiences for fans, encouraging user-generated content and discussions.
- **Press Tours:** The cast and crew participated in a global press tour, appearing on talk shows, podcasts, and at fan events, which helped maintain momentum and interest leading up to the release.

Critical Reception and Its Effect

Critical reception often plays a significant role in a film's box office performance. For "Joker: Folie à Deux," the reviews were largely positive, with particular praise for the performances, direction, and musical elements.

Critical Influence:

- **Positive Reviews:** High scores from critics on platforms like Rotten Tomatoes and Metacritic boosted audience confidence and encouraged more viewers to see the film.

- **Award Buzz:** Early buzz about potential awards for Phoenix and Gaga, as well as for direction and music, added a layer of prestige and drew in viewers who might typically wait for streaming releases.

Comparisons to Other Joker Films

The Joker, one of the most iconic villains in popular culture, has been portrayed by numerous actors across various films, each bringing a unique interpretation to the character. "Joker: Folie à Deux" continues this tradition, adding its own distinct flavor to the legacy of Gotham's Clown Prince of Crime. This chapter explores the similarities and differences between "Joker: Folie à Deux" and other notable Joker films, examining how each portrayal has influenced the character's enduring legacy.

"Joker" (2019) vs. "Joker: Folie à Deux"

Continuity and Evolution:

- **Narrative Continuity:** "Joker: Folie à Deux" directly follows the storyline established in "Joker" (2019), continuing the journey of Arthur Fleck. The sequel delves deeper into Arthur's psyche, further exploring his transformation into the Joker.

- **Character Evolution:** Joaquin Phoenix's portrayal of Arthur Fleck is a study in descent. In "Joker," he evolves from a downtrodden, mentally ill man into a symbol of chaos. In "Folie à Deux," his character is more entrenched in his Joker persona, exploring the consequences of his actions and his continued mental unraveling.

Thematic Parallels:

- **Mental Health:** Both films place a strong emphasis on mental health, portraying Arthur's struggles in a raw and unflinching manner. "Folie à Deux" expands on these themes, introducing new dimensions and perspectives on Arthur's condition.

- **Societal Commentary:** The original film critiques societal neglect and the consequences of alienation.

"Folie à Deux" builds on this foundation, examining the aftermath of Arthur's uprising and the broader impact on Gotham City.

"The Dark Knight" (2008) vs. "Joker: Folie à Deux"

Character Portrayal:

- **Heath Ledger's Joker:** In "The Dark Knight," Heath Ledger's Joker is a mysterious, anarchic force with an enigmatic background. His portrayal is chaotic and unpredictable, focused on disrupting the societal order.

- **Joaquin Phoenix's Joker:** Phoenix's Joker is more grounded, with a detailed backstory that humanizes him while exposing his darkness. "Folie à Deux" maintains this approach, delving further into his psyche and the complexities of his character.

Thematic Divergence:

- **Chaos vs. Tragedy:** Ledger's Joker embodies chaos without a clear motive, whereas Phoenix's Joker is a tragic figure whose descent into madness is both explained and empathetically portrayed. "Folie à Deux" continues to explore this tragic dimension, adding layers of depth and vulnerability to Arthur's character.

- **Societal Influence:** "The Dark Knight" presents the Joker as an agent of chaos testing Gotham's moral fiber. In contrast, "Folie à Deux" focuses more on personal and societal breakdowns, portraying how Arthur's actions resonate within a fractured society.

"Batman" (1989) vs. "Joker: Folie à Deux"

Character Interpretation:

- **Jack Nicholson's Joker:** Nicholson's portrayal is theatrical and flamboyant, blending dark humor with menace. His Joker is a crime lord with a penchant for showmanship.

- **Joaquin Phoenix's Joker:** Phoenix's interpretation is more subdued and psychological, eschewing flamboyance for a deeply personal and disturbing journey. "Folie à Deux" maintains this grounded approach, exploring Arthur's inner turmoil and his relationships.

Stylistic Differences:

- **Gothic vs. Realism:** Tim Burton's "Batman" features a gothic, stylized Gotham City, complementing Nicholson's exaggerated Joker. "Folie à Deux" continues the realistic, gritty aesthetic established in "Joker" (2019), portraying Gotham as a city grounded in real-world issues.
- **Tone and Atmosphere:** The tone of "Batman" (1989) is darkly comedic and fantastical, while "Folie à Deux" is intensely dramatic and psychological, with a focus on character-driven storytelling.

"Suicide Squad" (2016) vs. "Joker: Folie à Deux"

Character Design and Approach:

- **Jared Leto's Joker:** Leto's Joker in "Suicide Squad" is modern, stylized, and eccentric, characterized by tattoos and a gangster-like persona. His portrayal focuses on a more contemporary, volatile version of the character.
- **Joaquin Phoenix's Joker:** Phoenix's Joker is stripped of modern embellishments, focusing instead on the psychological horror of his transformation. "Folie à Deux" continues to explore this stripped-down, raw interpretation.

Narrative Focus:

- **Ensemble vs. Character Study:** "Suicide Squad" is an ensemble film with multiple storylines, where Joker is one of many characters. In contrast, "Folie à Deux" is a focused character study, deeply exploring Arthur Fleck's journey and the complexities of his mind.
- **Storytelling Style:** "Suicide Squad" employs a fast-paced, action-oriented narrative, whereas "Folie à Deux" adopts a slower, more introspective pace, emphasizing emotional depth and character development.

Influence on the Joker's Legacy

Shaping the Character:

- Each portrayal has added a unique layer to the Joker's legacy, reflecting the actor's interpretation and the film's thematic goals. Phoenix's Joker, particularly in "Folie à Deux," stands out for its intense focus on mental health and societal issues, presenting a deeply humanized and tragic villain.

Cultural Impact:

- The impact of each Joker film extends beyond the screen, influencing popular culture and public perception. Ledger's Joker became a cultural icon for chaos, Nicholson's for theatrical menace, Leto's for modern eccentricity, and Phoenix's for tragic realism.

Legacy of Adaptation:

- "Folie à Deux" builds on the legacy of its predecessors by continuing to push the boundaries of character exploration and thematic depth. It challenges audiences to confront uncomfortable truths about society, mental health, and the nature of evil.

Conclusion

"Joker: Folie à Deux" stands as a significant addition to the legacy of the Joker in film, offering a profound and unsettling exploration of the character. By comparing it to previous portrayals, we see how each interpretation has contributed to the evolving mythology of the Joker. From Ledger's chaotic anarchist to Phoenix's tragic anti-hero, the Joker continues to captivate and disturb, reflecting the darkest corners of the human psyche and society. As "Folie à Deux" continues to leave its mark, it reinforces the Joker's place as one of cinema's most complex and enduring villains.

Chapter 9: Impact and Legacy
Influence on Pop Culture

"Joker: Folie à Deux" has not only been a cinematic marvel but has also left an indelible mark on pop culture. This chapter delves into the multifaceted influence of the film on fashion, art, and various forms of media. As we explore the ripples it has created, we uncover a story that extends far beyond the silver screen, embedding itself deeply into the cultural fabric.

Fashion: A Dark Revolution

Costume Design and Iconic Looks:

- **Arthur's Transformation:** Joaquin Phoenix's Arthur Fleck, with his meticulously designed costumes, has inspired a surge in fashion trends. The sharp, yet disheveled look that epitomizes Arthur's descent into madness has been emulated by fashion designers worldwide. The iconic red suit, reminiscent of classic comic book hues yet grounded in a gritty reality, has become a symbol of rebellion and individuality.

- **Lady Gaga's Influence:** Lady Gaga's character, with her unique blend of elegance and eccentricity, has sparked a fashion revolution. Her costumes, often a blend of vintage glam and avant-garde, have influenced everything from high fashion runways to streetwear. Designers have taken cues from her bold choices, integrating elements of her style into their collections.

Runway to Street Style:

- **High Fashion:** Major fashion houses have embraced the film's aesthetic, incorporating dark, moody palettes, and dramatic silhouettes. Haute couture collections have featured pieces directly inspired by the movie, from the elaborate detailing to the

psychological undertones present in the designs.
- **Everyday Influence:** Beyond the runways, everyday fashion has seen a shift. Streetwear brands have launched collections that echo the film's themes, with graphic tees, tailored suits, and accessories that nod to the Joker's chaotic yet calculated style. This trend speaks to a broader cultural embrace of the film's ethos.

Art: Visual and Conceptual Resonance

Illustrations and Murals:

- **Urban Canvases:** Street artists have taken to urban landscapes, transforming walls into canvases that depict scenes from "Joker: Folie à Deux." Murals capturing Phoenix's haunting gaze or Lady Gaga's enigmatic presence have sprung up in cities worldwide, turning public spaces into galleries of homage.
- **Illustrative Impact:** Illustrators have been profoundly influenced by the film's visual storytelling. Comic book artists, in particular, have drawn inspiration from the movie's aesthetic, infusing their work with a similar intensity and emotional depth.

Fine Arts:

- **Gallery Exhibits:** Fine artists have embraced the film's themes, creating pieces that explore its psychological and societal commentary. Exhibitions have featured works that interpret the film's narrative through various mediums—paintings, sculptures, and installations—all resonating with the movie's dark, reflective tones.
- **Thematic Exploration:** The movie's exploration of identity, mental health, and societal breakdown has

provided rich material for conceptual artists. Pieces that delve into these themes, often abstract and thought-provoking, have been showcased in galleries, drawing parallels between the film and broader societal issues.

Media: A Ripple Effect

Film and Television:

- **Influence on Storytelling:** "Joker: Folie à Deux" has set a new benchmark for character-driven narratives in film and television. Its deep dive into the psyche of its protagonists has inspired a wave of similarly introspective and darkly thematic projects. Filmmakers and showrunners have been emboldened to explore complex characters and societal critiques, pushing the boundaries of conventional storytelling.

- **Cinematic Techniques:** The movie's innovative cinematography and visual style have influenced other directors and cinematographers. Techniques such as long takes, intense close-ups, and the use of color to convey emotion have been adopted and adapted in various productions, contributing to a richer visual language in contemporary cinema.

Music and Soundtracks:

- **Soundtrack Impact:** The haunting score of "Joker: Folie à Deux" has influenced musicians and composers, inspiring a wave of soundtracks that prioritize emotional resonance and psychological depth. The use of music as a narrative tool, integral to the storytelling, has become a trend, with more filmmakers recognizing the power of a compelling score.

- **Musical Homages:** Artists across genres have paid

homage to the film's music. Cover versions, remixes, and inspired compositions have flooded streaming platforms, reflecting the film's profound impact on the music industry.

Broader Cultural Phenomena

Mental Health Conversations:

- **Raising Awareness:** One of the most significant impacts of "Joker: Folie à Deux" is its contribution to the conversation around mental health. The film's raw portrayal of Arthur's struggles has sparked discussions on mental health issues, encouraging a more open and empathetic dialogue. Organizations and advocates have leveraged the film's popularity to promote awareness and support for mental health initiatives.

- **Influence on Other Media:** Books, articles, and documentaries examining mental health have drawn inspiration from the film's themes. The nuanced depiction of mental illness in the movie has set a new standard for how such topics are portrayed in media, promoting a more informed and compassionate approach.

Societal Reflection:

- **Mirror to Society:** The film's critique of societal neglect and the alienation of the marginalized has resonated deeply with audiences. It holds up a mirror to societal issues, prompting reflection and conversation. This resonance has extended to various cultural productions—literature, theater, and visual arts—that explore similar themes, creating a broader cultural dialogue on these critical issues.

- **Cultural Movements:** Movements advocating for social

justice and reform have found a powerful ally in the film's narrative. "Joker: Folie à Deux" has become a cultural touchstone for discussions on inequality, mental health, and societal responsibility, influencing public discourse and action.

Future of the Joker Franchise

As the credits roll on "Joker: Folie à Deux," fans and critics alike are left wondering: What's next for the Joker franchise? With its profound impact on pop culture and its reinvention of the iconic character, the future of the Joker is a topic ripe with speculation and anticipation. This chapter delves into potential sequels, spin-offs, and the possible directions the franchise might take, drawing from the latest available information and weaving together a tapestry of possibilities.

Potential Sequels: Expanding the Narrative

Continuation of Arthur Fleck's Story:

- **Deeper Descent:** A direct sequel to "Folie à Deux" could delve further into Arthur Fleck's psyche. Having fully embraced his identity as the Joker, Arthur's journey could explore new depths of madness and anarchy. The narrative might see him rising as a criminal mastermind, his actions increasingly impacting Gotham City and its residents.

- **Societal Chaos:** The societal upheaval sparked by Arthur's actions in the first two films could be further examined. A sequel might explore the broader consequences of his rebellion, showcasing the ripple effects on Gotham's social and political landscape. Themes of revolution, chaos, and the search for order in a disordered world could drive the plot.

Introducing New Characters:

- **Allies and Antagonists:** The introduction of new characters could add fresh dynamics to the story. Possible allies for the Joker, fellow outcasts or disillusioned individuals, might join his cause, amplifying the chaos. Alternatively, new antagonists, such as vigilantes or rival criminals, could emerge, challenging Arthur's dominance and pushing him to new extremes.

- **Harley Quinn:** While Lady Gaga's character in "Folie à Deux" remains a tantalizing mystery, her potential evolution into Harley Quinn is a storyline that fans are eager to see. A sequel could explore the complexities of their relationship, blending romance, madness, and violence in a narrative that further enriches both characters.

Spin-Offs: Expanding the Universe

Focus on Side Characters:

- **Character Origins:** Spin-offs focusing on the origins of side characters introduced in "Folie à Deux" could provide deeper insights into the Joker's world. Exploring their backstories and motivations would add layers to the franchise, offering fans a richer understanding of the universe.

- **Gotham's Underbelly:** A series or film centered on the various factions within Gotham's criminal underworld could provide a fascinating expansion. Characters such as gang leaders, corrupt officials, and other dark figures could take center stage, painting a broader picture of the chaos Arthur has unleashed.

Different Perspectives:

- **Victims and Survivors:** Spin-offs could also explore the perspectives of those affected by the Joker's actions. Stories focusing on victims, survivors, and their struggles to cope with the aftermath would provide a poignant counterbalance to the chaos. These narratives could highlight themes of resilience, revenge, and the search for justice.

- **Vigilante Justice:** The rise of vigilantes in response to the Joker's reign of terror could serve as compelling spin-off material. Characters inspired by or opposing the Joker could offer new angles on the story, exploring the moral ambiguities of taking justice into one's own hands.

Direction of the Franchise: Themes and Style

Dark Psychological Thrillers:

- **Maintaining Depth:** The franchise's success has largely stemmed from its deep psychological exploration of Arthur Fleck's character. Future films will likely continue to delve into the dark recesses of the human mind, maintaining the intense, introspective style that has become a hallmark of the series.

- **Complex Narratives:** Expect the franchise to maintain its complex, layered storytelling. Themes such as mental illness, identity, and societal decay will continue to be explored in nuanced and thought-provoking ways, challenging audiences to reflect on their own perceptions of morality and justice.

Evolution of Cinematic Techniques:

- **Visual Innovation:** The franchise's distinctive visual style, marked by its gritty realism and evocative cinematography, will likely evolve further. Future installments may experiment with new techniques, blending traditional filmmaking with innovative approaches to create a visually arresting experience.

- **Musical Integration:** The integration of music into the narrative, a standout element of "Folie à Deux," is expected to remain a key feature. Composers may explore new musical styles and motifs, using sound to enhance the emotional and psychological impact of the story.

Speculative Possibilities: Bold New Directions

Crossovers and Expanded Universes:

- **DC Universe Integration:** With the growing trend of cinematic universes, the Joker franchise might eventually integrate more closely with other DC properties. Crossovers with characters like Batman, Harley Quinn, or even other villains could provide fresh storylines and complex character interactions.

- **Standalone Stories:** Alternatively, the franchise could produce standalone stories that exist within the same universe but are not directly connected to Arthur Fleck. These films could explore different aspects of Gotham or introduce entirely new characters, maintaining the dark, psychological tone while expanding the scope of the narrative.

Exploration of Alternate Realities:

- **Multiverse Concepts:** Embracing the concept of the multiverse, the franchise could explore alternate realities and different versions of the Joker. This approach would allow for creative freedom, presenting radically different interpretations of the character and his world.

- **What-If Scenarios:** Films or series based on "what-if" scenarios—alternate outcomes of key events in Arthur's life—could provide fascinating explorations of character and fate. These stories could delve into the many paths not taken, offering a rich tapestry of possibilities.

Reflections on the Movie's Place in Cinema History

In the vast tapestry of cinema, certain films emerge not just as entertainment but as cultural landmarks, shaping the contours of art and society. "Joker: Folie à Deux" is poised to be one such film. As we reflect on its place in cinema history, we must consider its significance, its potential legacy, and how it will be remembered in the annals of film. Through this exploration, we aim to capture the essence of its impact, weaving a narrative that is both contemplative and profound.

Significance in Cinema

Reinventing the Superhero Genre:

- **Beyond Traditional Narratives:** "Joker: Folie à Deux" stands out for its daring departure from the conventional superhero film formula. Unlike its predecessors, it delves deep into the psyche of its protagonist, presenting a character study that is as unsettling as it is compelling. This focus on psychological complexity over action-driven plots has redefined what audiences can expect from a film based on comic book characters.

- **A Bold Artistic Vision:** The film's artistic approach, characterized by its gritty realism and unflinching portrayal of mental illness, sets it apart in a genre often dominated by fantastical elements. Its commitment to authenticity and its willingness to confront uncomfortable truths have elevated it to a work of cinematic art, resonating with viewers on a deeply personal level.

Impact on Filmmaking:

- **Innovative Techniques:** "Joker: Folie à Deux" has been lauded for its innovative use of cinematography and sound. The film's visual style, with its striking use of color and shadow, creates a haunting atmosphere that mirrors the protagonist's descent into madness. Similarly, the integration of music not just as background but as a narrative force has set a new standard for the use of sound in film.

- **Narrative Depth:** The film's layered storytelling, rich with symbolism and subtext, has challenged filmmakers to aspire to greater narrative complexity. It proves that audiences are not only capable of but hungry for stories that demand engagement and contemplation. This shift towards more intellectually and emotionally demanding content is a significant contribution to the evolution of modern cinema.

Legacy and Cultural Impact

Shaping Public Discourse:

- **Mental Health Awareness:** One of the most profound impacts of "Joker: Folie à Deux" is its contribution to the discourse on mental health. By portraying the struggles of its protagonist with raw honesty, the film has sparked conversations about the stigma and treatment of mental illness. Its depiction of the societal factors that contribute to individual suffering has fostered a greater understanding and empathy among viewers.

- **Reflection of Societal Issues:** The film's exploration of themes such as alienation, violence, and the breakdown of social structures mirrors contemporary societal anxieties. As a cultural artifact, it holds up a mirror to the times, prompting reflection and dialogue about the state of society and the human condition.

Influence on Future Filmmaking:

- **A New Standard for Character Studies:** The success of "Joker: Folie à Deux" is likely to inspire a wave of character-driven films that prioritize psychological depth and emotional resonance over spectacle. Filmmakers may take bolder risks in exploring the darker and more complex aspects of human nature, knowing that audiences are receptive to such narratives.

- **Encouraging Artistic Risk:** The film's critical and commercial success has demonstrated that there is a place in mainstream cinema for unconventional, artistically ambitious projects. This could lead to a broader acceptance of diverse storytelling approaches and encourage studios to support more innovative and experimental films.

How It Might Be Remembered

A Cultural Milestone:

- **Defining a Generation:** Just as certain films become emblematic of their time, "Joker: Folie à Deux" is likely to be remembered as a defining work of its era. Its themes, style, and impact on public consciousness position it as a cultural milestone that captures the spirit and struggles of the early 21st century.

- **A Touchstone for Future Films:** Future filmmakers will undoubtedly look to "Joker: Folie à Deux" as a touchstone, drawing inspiration from its approach to storytelling, character development, and thematic exploration. It will serve as a benchmark for excellence in psychological drama and character study.

Lasting Influence on Popular Culture:

- **Iconic Performances:** Joaquin Phoenix's portrayal of

Arthur Fleck/Joker and Lady Gaga's significant role will be remembered as career-defining performances that pushed the boundaries of acting. Their work in this film has set new standards for character embodiment and emotional depth, leaving a lasting legacy in the world of cinema.

- **Cultural References:** As with many seminal films, "Joker: Folie à Deux" will likely permeate popular culture, referenced in various forms of media and continuing to influence art, fashion, and even language. Its impact will extend beyond the screen, becoming a part of the cultural lexicon.

Conclusion

Final Thoughts

As we draw the curtains on our exploration of "Joker: Folie à Deux," it becomes evident that this film is more than a sequel—it is a profound artistic statement, a cultural touchstone, and a beacon of narrative innovation. Through its intricate layers, the film has woven a tapestry of themes and characters that invite us to reflect on the human condition, societal structures, and the very essence of identity.

Reinventing the Narrative: "Joker: Folie à Deux" dared to transcend the boundaries of its genre, crafting a narrative that is both introspective and expansive. By delving into the psyche of Arthur Fleck, the film offered a poignant character study that resonated deeply with audiences. It challenged us to see beyond the surface, to understand the complexities of mental illness and societal alienation. This psychological depth has redefined what a superhero—or in this case, supervillain—film can be, setting a new standard for character-driven storytelling.

Artistic Vision and Innovation: The film's success can be attributed to the uncompromising vision of its creative team. Director Todd Phillips, known for his unique approach to storytelling, brought a raw and authentic aesthetic to the film. His direction, combined with the screenplay's intricate layers, created a narrative that is as thought-provoking as it is emotionally charged. The cinematography, with its haunting visuals and meticulous attention to detail, and the evocative soundtrack, which serves as a narrative force in itself, further enriched the film's immersive experience.

Performances that Define a Generation: Central to the film's impact are the performances of its lead actors. Joaquin Phoenix's portrayal of Arthur Fleck/Joker is nothing short of transformative. His ability to embody the character's fragility, rage, and ultimate descent into madness is a testament to his extraordinary talent. Similarly, Lady Gaga's role added a new dimension to the narrative, her performance both powerful and nuanced, leaving an indelible mark on the film. Their portrayals have not only elevated the film but have also set new benchmarks for acting in cinema.

Cultural Impact and Legacy: The influence of "Joker: Folie à Deux" extends far beyond the screen. It has sparked important conversations about mental health, societal dynamics, and the nature of identity. Its themes have resonated deeply with viewers, prompting a broader dialogue about the issues it portrays. The film's cultural impact is evident in its influence on fashion, art, and media, where it continues to inspire and provoke thought.

Summarizing the Journey

Throughout this book, we have traversed the landscape of "Joker: Folie à Deux," examining its development, production, thematic elements, and reception. We have seen how the film was meticulously crafted from its inception to its release, with every element—from the creative team to the filming techniques—playing a crucial role in its success. We have delved into the characters, exploring the depth and nuance of their portrayals, and have analyzed the psychological and musical themes that enrich the narrative.

We have also looked at the broader impact of the film, considering its place in pop culture, its influence on future filmmaking, and its potential legacy. The fan theories, speculations, and audience expectations have shown us the enthusiasm and anticipation that surround the film. The critical reception and box office performance have provided insight into its commercial success and critical acclaim.

A Pivotal Moment in Cinema: "Joker: Folie à Deux" represents a pivotal moment in the history of cinema. It has challenged conventions, pushed artistic boundaries, and redefined what a film based on a comic book character can achieve. It stands as a testament to the power of storytelling, the importance of artistic vision, and the enduring appeal of complex, multifaceted characters.

Looking to the Future: As we look to the future, the legacy of "Joker: Folie à Deux" will continue to unfold. It will undoubtedly inspire future filmmakers to take bold creative risks, to explore deeper themes, and to craft narratives that resonate on a profound level. The film's impact on pop culture will persist, influencing new generations of artists and creators.

Reflecting on the Film's Significance

In the final analysis, "Joker: Folie à Deux" is a film that invites us to reflect—not just on the story it tells, but on the broader implications of its themes and characters. It asks us to consider the nature of identity, the impact of societal structures, and the complexities of mental health. It challenges us to empathize with its protagonist, to see the world through his eyes, and to understand the factors that shape his journey.

A Film That Resonates: The film's resonance lies in its ability to evoke a wide range of emotions—from empathy and compassion to discomfort and introspection. It is a film that stays with you, prompting reflection long after the credits roll. Its narrative, performances, and thematic depth ensure that it will be remembered as a landmark in cinema history.

A Lasting Impression: Ultimately, "Joker: Folie à Deux" leaves a lasting impression not just as a piece of entertainment, but as a work of art that speaks to the human experience. It is a film that challenges, provokes, and inspires, inviting us to see the world from a different perspective. Its significance, legacy, and impact will be felt for years to come, solidifying its place in the pantheon of great films.

As we conclude this journey, we are reminded of the power of storytelling to illuminate, to challenge, and to transform. "Joker: Folie à Deux" is a testament to that power, a film that stands as a beacon of artistic innovation and narrative depth. It is a film that, like the Joker himself, will continue to captivate, to intrigue, and to provoke thought in the hearts and minds of its audience.

What to Expect Next

As we stand at the crossroads of "Joker: Folie à Deux" and the boundless horizon of the future, it's impossible not to speculate with eager anticipation about what lies ahead for the Joker franchise. This film, a masterstroke of cinematic artistry, has not only expanded the boundaries of what a comic book adaptation can be but also carved out a significant place in contemporary culture. But what comes next? What new paths might this iconic character traverse? Let us venture into the realm of possibilities, exploring potential developments, future films, and the ongoing cultural relevance of the Joker.

Potential Developments

A Third Installment: The success of "Joker" and "Folie à Deux" sets the stage for a potential third installment. If a trilogy is on the horizon, what themes might it explore? Given the psychological depth and societal critique that defined its predecessors, a third film could delve even deeper into Arthur Fleck's psyche. Perhaps we will see him grappling with the consequences of his actions, exploring the ultimate collapse of his fractured identity, or even encountering new adversaries who mirror his own complexities.

Exploring New Narratives: Beyond a direct sequel, the universe of the Joker offers a plethora of narrative avenues. We might witness standalone stories that explore different facets of Gotham's underbelly, each with its own unique tone and style. These films could introduce new characters, expanding the lore and providing fresh perspectives on the chaos and order that define this world. Spin-offs focusing on supporting characters, such as Lady Gaga's enigmatic role, could offer deeper insights and rich, character-driven tales.

Innovative Storytelling Techniques: Given the innovative storytelling techniques employed in "Folie à Deux," future films might continue to push the boundaries of narrative and form. Musical elements, psychological explorations, and unconventional storytelling could become hallmarks of the franchise, creating a distinctive cinematic experience that challenges and captivates audiences. The blending of genres and the integration of music and visual art could elevate the storytelling to new heights, making each film a unique, immersive experience.

Future Films

Darker and More Introspective: Future films could venture into even darker and more introspective territories. Exploring themes such as existential despair, moral ambiguity, and the nature of evil could provide fertile ground for storytelling. These films could offer a nuanced portrayal of the Joker, moving beyond the binary of hero and villain to present a multifaceted character study that resonates with contemporary audiences.

Expanding the Gotham Universe: While the Joker remains the focal point, expanding the Gotham universe to include other iconic characters could enrich the narrative landscape. Imagine films that delve into the backstories of characters like Harley Quinn, Riddler, or Penguin, each offering a unique perspective on the world of Gotham. These interconnected stories could create a complex, layered cinematic universe that mirrors the intricate web of relationships and rivalries that define the comic book world.

Crossovers and Collaborations: In an era where crossovers have become a significant part of cinematic storytelling, the Joker franchise could explore collaborations with other characters from the DC universe. These crossovers could introduce new dynamics, conflicts, and alliances, providing fresh narrative opportunities. The interplay between the Joker and characters like Batman, Catwoman, or even lesser-known figures could lead to compelling and unpredictable storylines.

Ongoing Cultural Relevance

A Cultural Phenomenon: "Joker: Folie à Deux" has solidified the Joker as more than just a character—he is a cultural phenomenon. His influence extends beyond cinema into fashion, music, art, and social discourse. The character's complexity and the film's themes resonate with contemporary societal issues, ensuring that the Joker remains relevant and thought-provoking.

Inspiring New Creators: The film's success and innovative approach will undoubtedly inspire a new generation of filmmakers, writers, and artists. Its impact will be seen in the creation of bold, unconventional stories that challenge norms and push creative boundaries. The Joker's legacy will be carried forward by those who dare to explore the darker, more complex aspects of the human experience.

Conversations on Mental Health: One of the most significant impacts of the Joker films is the conversation they have sparked around mental health. By portraying the Joker's struggles with authenticity and empathy, the films have highlighted the importance of understanding and addressing mental health issues. This ongoing dialogue will continue to influence how mental health is represented in media and how society approaches these critical issues.

The Everlasting Appeal of the Joker

A Timeless Character: The Joker's appeal lies in his timelessness. He embodies chaos, unpredictability, and the darker side of human nature—qualities that are perpetually relevant. As society evolves, the Joker adapts, reflecting contemporary fears, desires, and conflicts. This adaptability ensures that the character remains a compelling figure, constantly reinvented for new generations.

Myth and Archetype: In many ways, the Joker has transcended his origins to become a mythic archetype. He represents the trickster, the agent of chaos, challenging the status quo and exposing underlying truths. This archetypal role ensures that the Joker will continue to captivate audiences, providing a mirror through which we can examine ourselves and our world.

Endless Storytelling Potential: The richness of the Joker's character offers endless storytelling potential. Each new interpretation adds layers to his mythos, allowing for infinite exploration. Whether through film, television, literature, or other media, the Joker's story will continue to evolve, surprising and engaging audiences with each new iteration.

A Hopeful Future

As we look to the future of the Joker franchise, there is much to be hopeful for. The films have set a high standard for storytelling, creativity, and thematic depth, paving the way for future projects to build upon this foundation. The cultural impact of "Joker: Folie à Deux" will continue to resonate, inspiring new stories and discussions.

In this evolving landscape, the Joker remains a symbol of the complexity and unpredictability of the human condition. His journey, marked by moments of madness, genius, and profound insight, will continue to intrigue and inspire. The future of the Joker franchise is not just about the next film or story—it's about the ongoing exploration of what it means to be human, seen through the eyes of one of fiction's most enigmatic characters.

As we conclude this chapter, we do so with a sense of anticipation and excitement. The Joker's story is far from over, and the future holds countless possibilities. In the spirit of Neil Gaiman's storytelling, we embrace the unknown, ready to be surprised, challenged, and inspired by whatever comes next in the saga of the Joker.

Appendices
Key Interviews and Quotes

Joaquin Phoenix on Returning as the Joker

In a candid interview with *Variety*, Joaquin Phoenix shared his thoughts on reprising his role as Arthur Fleck in "Joker: Folie à Deux." He reflected on the profound impact the character had on him and the complexities involved in returning to such a dark, layered role.

"Arthur is a character that stays with you, long after the cameras stop rolling. Coming back to him meant diving even deeper into his psyche, exploring new facets of his madness and humanity. It was both daunting and exhilarating."

Phoenix's dedication to authenticity shines through as he discusses his preparation for the sequel:

"I spent months researching, reading, and working with Todd [Phillips] to ensure that every aspect of Arthur's journey felt true to the character we created. It's a relentless process, but it's what makes portraying the Joker so uniquely challenging and rewarding."

Lady Gaga on Her Character

In an exclusive interview with *The Hollywood Reporter*, Lady Gaga opened up about her role in the film and the creative process behind her character.

"Joining the 'Joker' universe was a transformative experience. My character is intricately woven into Arthur's story, and it was essential to bring a depth and complexity that complements Joaquin's performance. We wanted to create something that felt raw and real."

She further elaborated on her preparation:

"I immersed myself in the world of my character, understanding her motivations and struggles. It's not just about playing a part;

it's about living it. The synergy between music and performance was key, and Todd encouraged me to infuse elements of my musical background into the role."

Director Todd Phillips on His Vision

In a detailed discussion with *Deadline*, director Todd Phillips shared his vision for "Joker: Folie à Deux" and how it evolved from the first film.

"The first 'Joker' was about the origin, the spark that ignites chaos. With 'Folie à Deux,' we wanted to delve into the aftermath, exploring the consequences of Arthur's transformation and how it reverberates through his psyche and the world around him."

Phillips highlighted the collaborative nature of the project:

"Working with Joaquin and Gaga was a symbiotic process. Their insights and creative input were invaluable in shaping the narrative and emotional arcs. The goal was to push boundaries and create something that resonates on a visceral level with the audience."

Hildur Guðnadóttir on Composing the Soundtrack

In an interview with *Rolling Stone*, composer Hildur Guðnadóttir discussed her approach to the film's soundtrack and the challenges of capturing its emotional depth.

"The music for 'Folie à Deux' needed to reflect the duality of the characters and the chaos within. I experimented with dissonance and harmony, creating a soundscape that mirrors the turmoil and beauty of Arthur's world. Each track is a piece of the puzzle, contributing to the overall narrative."

Guðnadóttir also spoke about the collaborative process with the filmmakers:

"Todd and I worked closely to ensure that the music was an integral part of the storytelling. It wasn't just about background scores but about creating moments where the music speaks as loudly as the dialogue or the silence."

Critic Reviews and Insights

Early reviews from prominent critics provide a spectrum of insights into "Joker: Folie à Deux." In *The New York Times*, critic A.O. Scott praised the film's ambition and emotional depth:

"'Folie à Deux' is a haunting symphony of chaos and despair, elevated by Phoenix and Gaga's electrifying performances. It's a testament to the enduring power of the Joker as a cultural icon, pushing the boundaries of what a comic book film can achieve."

Conversely, *The Guardian*'s Peter Bradshaw offered a more tempered view:

"While 'Folie à Deux' is visually stunning and thematically ambitious, it occasionally falters under the weight of its own aspirations. However, the performances are undeniably compelling, making it a worthy follow-up to its predecessor."

Todd Phillips on the Challenges of Filming

In an interview with *IndieWire*, Todd Phillips discussed the logistical challenges faced during production and how they overcame them:

"Filming 'Folie à Deux' was an intense process. We faced numerous logistical hurdles, from location constraints to tight schedules. But the passion and dedication of the cast and crew were extraordinary. Every challenge was met with creativity and resilience, resulting in a film that we're immensely proud of."

Phillips also reflected on the collaborative spirit on set:

"There was a sense of camaraderie and mutual respect that fueled the entire process. Joaquin and Gaga brought their A-game every day, and their commitment was contagious. It's this collective effort that made 'Folie à Deux' such a unique and powerful experience."

Lady Gaga on Her Collaborative Process

Speaking with *Entertainment Weekly*, Lady Gaga elaborated on her collaborative process with Joaquin Phoenix and Todd Phillips:

"Working with Joaquin is like a dance. There's a rhythm and flow to our scenes that comes from deep trust and mutual respect. Todd's direction was the guiding light, ensuring that every moment was truthful and impactful. It was a transformative journey, one that I'm incredibly grateful for."

Joaquin Phoenix on the Film's Impact

In a reflective interview with *Collider*, Joaquin Phoenix discussed the film's impact and its place in his career:

"'Folie à Deux' is more than a sequel; it's a continuation of a journey that explores the darkest corners of the human soul. It's a film that challenges and provokes, forcing both the characters and the audience to confront uncomfortable truths. For me, it's been a profound and deeply personal experience."

These interviews and quotes offer a multifaceted view of "Joker: Folie à Deux," shedding light on the creative minds behind the film and their journey to bring this complex narrative to life. As we reflect on their words, we gain a deeper understanding of the film's significance and the collaborative effort that made it a reality.

Additional Resources and Reading

For those captivated by "Joker: Folie à Deux" and eager to delve deeper into the world of the Joker, a wealth of resources is available. From academic analyses to behind-the-scenes documentaries, these recommendations will enrich your understanding and appreciation of this complex character and the film's intricate narrative.

Books

1. **"The Killing Joke" by Alan Moore and Brian Bolland**
    - A seminal graphic novel that delves into the Joker's origin story, "The Killing Joke" offers a dark and thought-provoking exploration of his psyche. Alan Moore's storytelling, combined with Brian Bolland's stark artwork, makes this an essential read for any Joker enthusiast.

2. **"Batman: The Dark Knight Returns" by Frank Miller**
    - While primarily focused on Batman, Frank Miller's graphic novel presents a chilling depiction of the Joker. The story's mature themes and gritty tone have heavily influenced modern portrayals of the character, including those seen in the recent films.

3. **"Joker: A Visual History of the Clown Prince of Crime" by Daniel Wallace**
    - This comprehensive visual guide chronicles the evolution of the Joker across various media. Featuring artwork, character designs, and behind-the-scenes insights, it's a treasure trove for fans interested in the Joker's cultural impact.

4. **"The Man Who Laughs" by Victor Hugo**

- Though not directly about the Joker, Victor Hugo's novel is widely regarded as an inspiration for the character. The story of Gwynplaine, a disfigured man whose perpetual grin mirrors the Joker's, provides a fascinating historical context for understanding the origins of the iconic villain.

Articles and Essays

1. **"The Philosophy of the Joker" by Mark D. White and Robert Arp**
   - Published in *The Atlantic*, this article delves into the philosophical implications of the Joker's actions and ideology. It's a compelling read for those interested in the deeper ethical and moral questions posed by the character.

2. **"The Joker's Wild: A Psychological Analysis" by Dr. Travis Langley**
   - Featured in *Psychology Today*, this piece explores the psychological profile of the Joker, examining his mental disorders and their manifestations. Dr. Langley's analysis provides a clinical perspective on the character's complex behavior.

3. **"Behind the Mask: The Evolution of the Joker in Film" by Emily Todd VanDerWerff**
   - This *Vox* article traces the Joker's cinematic journey, comparing different portrayals and their cultural significance. It's an insightful read for those interested in the character's transformation on the big screen.

Documentaries and Videos

1. **"The Making of Joker"**
   - This behind-the-scenes documentary offers

an in-depth look at the creation of the 2019 film "Joker," featuring interviews with the cast and crew. It's a must-watch for fans of Todd Phillips' vision and Joaquin Phoenix's performance.

2. **"Batman & Bill"**
    - Available on Hulu, this documentary tells the story of Bill Finger, the co-creator of Batman and, by extension, the Joker. It sheds light on the often-overlooked contributions of Finger to the Batman mythos and the creation of one of its most iconic villains.

3. **"The Mind of a Villain: The Joker"**
    - A video essay available on YouTube that analyzes the Joker's character across different media. It delves into the psychological and narrative aspects that make the Joker a compelling and enduring antagonist.

4. **"The Joker: History of a Sociopath"**
    - This documentary, available on various streaming platforms, explores the real-life inspirations and psychological theories behind the Joker. It's a comprehensive examination of how the character has been shaped by and reflects societal fears and fascinations.

Academic Papers

1. **"Clowning Around: The Joker and the Performance of Violence" by Dr. Rachel Caine**
    - Published in the *Journal of Popular Culture*, this paper explores the performative nature of the Joker's violence and its implications within the context of media studies. Dr. Caine's work provides a scholarly perspective

on the character's impact.

2. **"Joker as Anti-Hero: A Study in Comic Book Narratives" by Dr. Jonathan Gray**
    - This academic paper, available through university libraries, examines the Joker's role as an anti-hero in modern comics. Dr. Gray's analysis highlights the complexities and contradictions inherent in the character.

3. **"The Dark Side of Comedy: The Joker's Legacy in Popular Culture" by Dr. Amanda Green**
    - Featured in the *International Journal of Cultural Studies*, this paper discusses the Joker's role as a dark comedic figure and its influence on contemporary media. Dr. Green's research offers a cultural studies perspective on the character.

Websites and Online Resources

1. **The Joker's Lair (thejokerslair.com)**
    - A fan site dedicated to all things Joker, featuring news, articles, and forums for discussion. It's a great resource for staying up-to-date with the latest developments and fan theories.

2. **Batman Wiki (batman.fandom.com)**
    - This comprehensive wiki covers everything about the Batman universe, including detailed pages on the Joker's various incarnations. It's an invaluable resource for fans seeking detailed information and trivia.

3. **DC Universe Infinite (dcuniverseinfinite.com)**
    - DC Comics' official digital platform offers access to a vast library of Joker comics, from classic issues to modern stories. Subscribing to this service allows fans to explore the

character's evolution in the comics.

By diving into these resources, readers can gain a richer and more nuanced understanding of "Joker: Folie à Deux" and its place within the broader tapestry of the Joker's legacy. Whether through academic analyses, engaging documentaries, or in-depth articles, each resource offers a unique perspective on the enduring enigma of the Clown Prince of Crime.

Printed in Great Britain
by Amazon